C++ FOR DUMMIES®

Quick Reference

by Namir Clement Shammas

IDG
BOOKS
WORLDWIDE

IDG Books Worldwide, Inc.
An International Data Group Company

Foster City, CA ✦ Chicago, IL ✦ Indianapolis, IN ✦ Southlake, TX

C++ For Dummies® Quick Reference

Published by
IDG Books Worldwide, Inc.
An International Data Group Company
919 E. Hillsdale Blvd.
Suite 400
Foster City, CA 94404
www.idgbooks.com (IDG Books Worldwide Web site)
www.dummies.com (Dummies Press Web site)

Library of Congress Catalog Card No.: 97-73303

ISBN: 0-7645-0246-8

Printed in the United States of America

10 9 8 7 6 5 4 3 2 1

1A/SZ/QX/ZX/IN

Distributed in the United States by IDG Books Worldwide, Inc.

Distributed by Macmillan Canada for Canada; by Transworld Publishers Limited in the United Kingdom; by IDG Norge Books for Norway; by IDG Sweden Books for Sweden; by Woodslane Pty. Ltd. for Australia; by Woodslane Enterprises Ltd. for New Zealand; by Longman Singapore Publishers Ltd. for Singapore, Malaysia, Thailand, and Indonesia; by Simron Pty. Ltd. for South Africa; by Toppan Company Ltd. for Japan; by Distribuidora Cuspide for Argentina; by Livraria Cultura for Brazil; by Ediciencia S.A. for Ecuador; by Addison-Wesley Publishing Company for Korea; by Ediciones ZETA S.C.R. Ltda. for Peru; by WS Computer Publishing Corporation, Inc., for the Philippines; by Unalis Corporation for Taiwan; by Contemporanea de Ediciones for Venezuela; by Computer Book & Magazine Store for Puerto Rico; by Express Computer Distributors for the Caribbean and West Indies. Authorized Sales Agent: Anthony Rudkin Associates for the Middle East and North Africa.

For general information on IDG Books Worldwide's books in the U.S., please call our Consumer Customer Service department at 800-762-2974. For reseller information, including discounts and premium sales, please call our Reseller Customer Service department at 800-434-3422.

For information on where to purchase IDG Books Worldwide's books outside the U.S., please contact our International Sales department at 415-655-3200 or fax 415-655-3295.

For information on foreign language translations, please contact our Foreign & Subsidiary Rights department at 415-655-3021 or fax 415-655-3281.

For sales inquiries and special prices for bulk quantities, please contact our Sales department at 415-655-3200 or write to the address above.

For information on using IDG Books Worldwide's books in the classroom or for ordering examination copies, please contact our Educational Sales department at 800-434-2086 or fax 817-251-8174.

For press review copies, author interviews, or other publicity information, please contact our Public Relations department at 415-655-3000 or fax 415-655-3299.

For authorization to photocopy items for corporate, personal, or educational use, please contact Copyright Clearance Center, 222 Rosewood Drive, Danvers, MA 01923, or fax 508-750-4470.

About the Author

Namir Clement Shammas is a full-time author who specializes in object-oriented programming and Windows programming books. He has written and coauthored more than 60 programming books, including *Object-Oriented Programming For Dummies* (published by IDG Books Worldwide, Inc.). Namir holds B.S. and M.S. degrees in chemical engineering.

ABOUT IDG BOOKS WORLDWIDE

Welcome to the world of IDG Books Worldwide.

IDG Books Worldwide, Inc., is a subsidiary of International Data Group, the world's largest publisher of computer-related information and the leading global provider of information services on information technology. IDG was founded more than 25 years ago and now employs more than 8,500 people worldwide. IDG publishes more than 275 computer publications in over 75 countries (see listing below). More than 60 million people read one or more IDG publications each month.

Launched in 1990, IDG Books Worldwide is today the #1 publisher of best-selling computer books in the United States. We are proud to have received eight awards from the Computer Press Association in recognition of editorial excellence and three from *Computer Currents'* First Annual Readers' Choice Awards. Our best-selling *...For Dummies*® series has more than 30 million copies in print with translations in 30 languages. IDG Books Worldwide, through a joint venture with IDG's Hi-Tech Beijing, became the first U.S. publisher to publish a computer book in the People's Republic of China. In record time, IDG Books Worldwide has become the first choice for millions of readers around the world who want to learn how to better manage their businesses.

Our mission is simple: Every one of our books is designed to bring extra value and skill-building instructions to the reader. Our books are written by experts who understand and care about our readers. The knowledge base of our editorial staff comes from years of experience in publishing, education, and journalism — experience we use to produce books for the '90s. In short, we care about books, so we attract the best people. We devote special attention to details such as audience, interior design, use of icons, and illustrations. And because we use an efficient process of authoring, editing, and desktop publishing our books electronically, we can spend more time ensuring superior content and spend less time on the technicalities of making books.

You can count on our commitment to deliver high-quality books at competitive prices on topics you want to read about. At IDG Books Worldwide, we continue in the IDG tradition of delivering quality for more than 25 years. You'll find no better book on a subject than one from IDG Books Worldwide.

John Kilcullen
CEO
IDG Books Worldwide, Inc.

Steven Berkowitz
President and Publisher
IDG Books Worldwide, Inc.

IDG Books Worldwide, Inc., is a subsidiary of International Data Group, the world's largest publisher of computer-related information and the leading global provider of information services on information technology. International Data Group publishes over 275 computer publications in over 75 countries. Sixty million people read one or more International Data Group publications each month. International Data Group's publications include: ARGENTINA: Buyer's Guide, Computerworld Argentina, PC World Argentina; AUSTRALIA: Australian Macworld, Australian PC World, Australian Reseller News, Computerworld, IT Casebook, Network World, Publish, Webmaster; AUSTRIA: Computerwelt Osterreich, Networks Austria, PC Tip Austria; BANGLADESH: PC World Bangladesh; BELARUS: PC World Belarus; BELGIUM: Data News; BRAZIL: Annuario de Informática, Computerworld, Connections, Macworld, PC Player, PC World, Publish, Reseller News, Supergamepower; BULGARIA: Computerworld Bulgaria, Network World Bulgaria, PC & MacWorld Bulgaria; CANADA: CIO Canada, Client/Server World, ComputerWorld Canada, InfoWorld Canada, NetworkWorld Canada, WebWorld; CHILE: Computerworld Chile, PC World Chile; COLOMBIA: Computerworld Colombia, PC World Colombia; COSTA RICA: PC World Centro America; THE CZECH AND SLOVAK REPUBLICS: Computerworld Czechoslovakia, Macworld Czech Republic, PC World Czechoslovakia; DENMARK: Communications World Danmark, Computerworld Danmark, Macworld Danmark, PC World Danmark, Techworld Denmark; DOMINICAN REPUBLIC: PC World Republica Dominicana; ECUADOR: PC World Ecuador; EGYPT: Computerworld Middle East, PC World Middle East; EL SALVADOR: PC World Centro America; FINLAND: MikroPC, Tietoverkko, Tietoviikko; FRANCE: Distributique, Hebdo, Info PC, Le Monde Informatique, Macworld, Reseaux & Telecoms, WebMaster France; GERMANY: Computer Partner, Computerwoche, Computerwoche Extra, Computerwoche FOCUS, Global Online, Macwelt, PC Welt; GREECE: Amiga Computing, GamePro Greece, Multimedia World; GUATEMALA: PC World Centro America; HONDURAS: PC World Centro America; HONG KONG: Computerworld Hong Kong, PC World Hong Kong, Publish in Asia; HUNGARY: ABCD CD-ROM, Computerworld Szamitastechnika, Internetto online Magazine, PC World Hungary, PC-X Magazin Hungary; ICELAND: Tolvuheimur PC World Island; INDIA: Information Communications World, Information Systems Computerworld, PC World India, Publish in Asia; INDONESIA: InfoKomputer PC World, Komputek Computerworld, Publish in Asia; IRELAND: ComputerScope, PC Live!; ISRAEL: Macworld Israel, People & Computers/Computerworld; ITALY: Computerworld Italia, Macworld Italia, Networking Italia, PC World Italia; JAPAN: DTP World, Macworld Japan, Nikkei Personal Computing, OS/2 World Japan, SunWorld Japan, Windows NT World, Windows World Japan; KENYA: PC World East African; KOREA: Hi-Tech Information, Macworld Korea, PC World Korea; MACEDONIA: PC World Macedonia; MALAYSIA: Computerworld Malaysia, PC World Malaysia, Publish in Asia; MALTA: PC World Malta; MEXICO: Computerworld Mexico, PC World Mexico; MYANMAR: PC World Myanmar; NETHERLANDS: Computer! Totaal, LAN Internetworking Magazine, LAN World Buyers Guide, Macworld Netherlands, Net, WebWereld; NEW ZEALAND: Absolute Beginners Guide and Plain & Simple Series, Computer Buyer, Computer Industry Directory, Computerworld New Zealand, MTB, Network World, PC World New Zealand; NICARAGUA: PC World Centro America; NORWAY: Computerworld Norge, CW Rapport, Datamagasinet, Financial Rapport, Kursguide Norge, Macworld Norge, Multimediaworld Norge, PC World Ekspress Norge, PC World Nettverk, PC World Norge, PC World ProduktGuide Norge; PAKISTAN: Computerworld Pakistan; PANAMA: PC World Panama; PEOPLE'S REPUBLIC OF CHINA: China Computer Users, China Computerworld, China InfoWorld, China Telecom World Weekly, Computer & Communication, Electronic Design China, Electronics Today, Electronics Weekly, Game Software, PC World China, Popular Computer Week, Software Weekly, Software World, Telecom World; PERU: Computerworld Peru, PC World Profesional Peru, PC World SoHo Peru; PHILIPPINES: Click!, Computerworld Philippines, PC World Philippines, Publish in Asia; POLAND: Computerworld Poland, Computerworld Special Report Poland, Cyber, Macworld Poland, Networld Poland, PC World Komputer; PORTUGAL: Cerebro/PC World, Computerworld/Correio Informático, Dealer World Portugal, Mac*In/PC*In Portugal, Multimedia World; PUERTO RICO: PC World Puerto Rico; ROMANIA: Computerworld Romania, PC World Romania, Telecom Romania; RUSSIA: Computerworld Russia, Mir PK, Publish, Seti; SINGAPORE: Computerworld Singapore, PC World Singapore, Publish in Asia; SLOVENIA: Monitor; SOUTH AFRICA: Computing SA, Network World SA, Software World SA; SPAIN: Communications World España, Computerworld España, Dealer World España, Macworld España, PC World España; SRI LANKA: Infolink PC World; SWEDEN: CAP&Design, Computer Sweden, Corporate Computing Sweden, Internetworld Sweden, it branschen, Macworld Sweden, MaxiData Sweden, MikroDatorn, Närverk & Kommunikation, PC World Sweden, PCaktiv, Windows World Sweden; SWITZERLAND: Computerworld Schweiz, Macworld Schweiz, PCtip; TAIWAN: Computerworld Taiwan, Macworld Taiwan, NEW ViSiON/Publish, PC World Taiwan, Windows World Taiwan; THAILAND: Publish in Asia, Thai Computerworld; TURKEY: Computerworld Turkiye, Macworld Turkiye, Network World Turkiye, PC World Turkiye; UKRAINE: Computerworld Kiev, Multimedia World Ukraine, PC World Ukraine; UNITED KINGDOM: Acorn User UK, Amiga Action UK, Amiga Computing UK, Apple Talk UK, Computing, Macworld, Parents and Computers UK, PC Advisor, PC Home, PSX Pro, The WEB; UNITED STATES: Cable in the Classroom, CIO Magazine, Computerworld, DOS World, Federal Computer Week, GamePro Magazine, InfoWorld, I-Way, Macworld, Network World, PC Games, PC World, Publish, Video Event, THE WEB Magazine, and WebMaster; online webzines: JavaWorld, NetscapeWorld, and SunWorld Online; URUGUAY: InfoWorld Uruguay; VENEZUELA: Computerworld Venezuela, PC World Venezuela; and VIETNAM: PC World Vietnam.   3/24/97

Dedication

To a special friend, Jane Bernard, for being there when the pain was unbearable. I'll miss you at the next Greek Food Festival!

Author's Acknowledgments

This book is the fruit of the efforts of many people. I want to thank Diane Steele, the associate publisher, and Leah Cameron, the editorial manager with this project, for sharing my vision in this book. Many thanks to my literary agent, Carol McLyndon of Waterside Productions, for encouraging me and pursuing this project. I also want to thank the technical editor, Garrett Pease, for his excellent work. Many thanks to the project editor, Robert Wallace, and the editors who worked on this book: John Edwards, Bill Barton, Patricia Pan, and Diane Giangrossi. They made valuable contributions to shaping this manuscript. Let's do it again soon!

Publisher's Acknowledgments

We're proud of this book; please send us your comments about it by using the Reader Response Card at the back of the book or by e-mailing us at feedback/dummies@idgbooks.com. Some of the people who helped bring this book to market include the following:

Acquisitions, Development, and Editorial

Project Editor: Robert H. Wallace

Senior Acquisitions Editor: Jill Pisoni

Copy Editors: John C. Edwards, Patricia Yuu Pan

Technical Editor: Garrett Pease

Editorial Manager: Leah P. Cameron

Editorial Assistant: Donna Love

Production

Project Coordinator: Valery Bourke

Layout and Graphics: Anna Rohrer, M. Anne Sipahimalani

Proofreaders: Ethel M. Winslow, Christine D. Berman, Joel K. Draper, Rachel Garvey, Robert Springer

Indexer: Sharon Hilgenberg

Special Help

Diane L. Giangrossi, Associate Editor/Quality Control; William A. Barton, Copy Editor; Linda Stark, Copy Editor

---

General and Administrative

IDG Books Worldwide, Inc.: John Kilcullen, CEO; Steven Berkowitz, President and Publisher

Dummies, Inc.: Brenda McLaughlin, Senior Vice President and Group Publisher

Dummies Technology Press and Dummies Editorial: Diane Graves Steele, Vice President and Associate Publisher; Judith A. Taylor, Product Marketing Manager; Kristin A. Cocks, Editorial Director

Dummies Trade Press: Kathleen A. Welton, Vice President and Publisher

IDG Books Production for Dummies Press: Beth Jenkins, Production Director; Cindy L. Phipps, Manager of Project Coordination, Production Proofreading, and Indexing; Kathie S. Schutte, Supervisor of Page Layout; Shelley Lea, Supervisor of Graphics and Design; Debbie J. Gates, Production Systems Specialist; Robert Springer, Supervisor of Proofreading; Debbie Stailey, Special Projects Coordinator; Tony Augsburger, Supervisor of Reprints and Bluelines; Leslie Popplewell, Media Archive Coordinator

Dummies Packaging and Book Design: Patti Sandez, Packaging Specialist; Kavish + Kavish, Cover Design

♦

The publisher would like to give special thanks to Patrick J. McGovern, without whom this book would not have been possible.

♦

Contents at a Glance

Introduction: How to Use This Book 1

Part I: Getting to Know C++ 5

Part II: Constants and Variables 17

Part III: Operators 27

Part IV: Input and Output (Streaming) 41

Part V: Decision-Making 49

Part VI: Loops 63

Part VII: Data Types, Enumerated
Types, and Data Structures 77

Part VIII: Arrays 99

Part IX: Pointers 115

Part X: Functions and Arguments 133

Part XI: Strings 149

Part XII: Classes 163

Part XIII: Advanced OOP 199

Glossary: Techie Talk 211

Index 215

IDG Books Worldwide Registration Card ..... Back of Book

Table of Contents

Introduction: How to Use This Book 1

How This Book Is Organized 2
Conventions Used in This Book 3
Icon Legend 4

Part I: Getting to Know C++ 5

About C++ Basics..6
A Simple C++ Program 6
Comments 8
Compiler Directives 8
    The #define directive...9
    The #error directive 10
    The #if and #elif directives 10
    The #ifdef and #ifndef directives 11
    The #include directive 13
    The #undef directive 13
Programs That Compile C++ 14
Rules for Naming Items 15
Special Characters 16

Part II: Constants and Variables.................. 17

Constants..18
    Naming conventions for constants 19
    Using constants 19
    Using type definitions 21
Reference Variables 22
Variables 23

Part III: Operators 27

Arithmetic Operators 28
Assignment Operators 28
Boolean and Relational Operators 29
Bit Manipulation Operators.......................................33
The Comma Operator 33
Decrement and Increment Operators 34
Dynamic Allocation Operators..................................35
    The operator new 36
    The operator delete 37
Pointer Operators 38
Sizeof Operator..38
Typecasting 39

Part IV: Input and Output (Streaming) 41

Basic Stream Input/Output 42
Common File Stream I/O Functions 42
   Close member function 42
   Open member function 43
   Other member functions 44
Random-Access Stream I/O 44
Sequential Binary Stream I/O 45
   Write member function 45
   Read member function 46
Sequential Text Stream I/O 47
Stream Library 48

Part V: Decision-Making 49

If Statement 50
If-Else Statement 52
Multiple-Alternative If Statement 54
Multiple-Alternative Switch Statement 58

Part VI: Loops 63

Do-While Loop 64
Exiting Loops 66
For Loop 68
Nesting Loops 71
Skipping Loop Iterations 73
While Loop 73

Part VII: Data Types, Enumerated
Types, and Data Structures 77

Data Types (Predefined) 78
   Boolean data type 78
   Character data type 78
   Floating-point data types 80
   Integer data types 83
   String data type 86
   Void data type 88
   Type definition in C++ 88
Enumerated Types 90
Structures 92
   Declaring structures 92
   Declaring structured variables 94

Accessing structure members 94
Initializing structures 95
Copying structured variables 96
Unions 97

Part VIII: Arrays 99

Dynamic Arrays 100
Multidimensional Arrays 103
Accessing multidimensional arrays 103
Declaring multidimensional arrays 104
Initializing multidimensional arrays 105
Single-Dimensional Arrays 110
Accessing single-dimensional arrays 110
Declaring single-dimensional arrays 110
Initializing single-dimensional arrays 111

Part IX: Pointers 115

Constant Pointers 116
Declaring Pointers 116
Declaring an Array of Function Pointers 117
Far Pointers 118
Initializing Pointers 119
Passing Arguments by Pointer 120
Pointers to enumerated types
as function parameters 120
Pointers to structures as function parameters 121
Pointers to functions as parameters 122
Passing Arrays as Function Parameters 123
Pointers to Arrays 124
Array names are pointers, too! 124
Pointer arithmetic 125
Array element access via pointers 125
Pointers to Existing Variables 126
Pointers to Functions 127
Pointers to Objects 129
Pointers to Pointers 130
Pointers to Structures 130
Reference Variables versus Pointers 131

Part X: Functions and Arguments 133

Arguments 134
Default arguments 134
Passing arguments by reference 135
Strings as arguments 136

Functions 137
   Exiting functions 137
   Inline functions 138
   Overloading 139
   Parameters of functions 140
   Prototyping functions 143
   Recursion 145
   Syntax 145
   Void functions 147

Part XI: Strings 149

About the STRING.H Library 150
Comparing Strings 150
   Strcmp function 150
   Stricmp function 151
   Strncmp function 152
   Strnicmp function 152
Concatenating Strings 153
   Strcat function 153
   Strncat function 153
Converting Strings 154
   Strupr function 154
   Strlwr function 155
Copying Strings 155
   Strcpy function 155
   Strncpy function 156
Finding Characters 156
   Strchr function 157
   Strrchr function 157
   Strspn function 158
   Strcspn function 159
Finding Substrings 160
Getting the Length of a String 160
Initializing Strings 161
Reversing Strings 161

Part XII: Classes 163

Constructors 164
Declaring Classes — the Basics 166
   Public section 169
   Protected section 170
   Private section 170
Declaring Objects (Or Class Instances) 172
Destructors 175
Exceptions 177
   Exception classes 177
   Standard exceptions 177

Throwing an exception 178
Try block 179
Catch clauses 180
Friend Functions 182
Member Functions 183
Nested Data Types 186
Nested classes 186
Nested enumerated types 187
Nested structures 190
Operators 191
Declaring operators 192
Friend operators 193
Static Members 194
Declaring static data members 195
Initializing static data members 196
Static member functions 197

Part XIII: Advanced OOP *199*

Abstract Classes 200
Declaring a Class Hierarchy 201
Multiple Inheritance 204
Namespace 206
Overloading Member Functions and Operators 207
Virtual Functions 207

Glossary: Techie Talk *211*

Index *215*

IDG Books Worldwide
Registration Card .... *Back of Book*

How to Use This Book

You know, you're pretty smart for buying a ...*For Dummies Quick Reference* that covers C++. I mean, like genius-level smart. You understand that all *you* need out of a book on C++ is a few reminders about how those strange, convoluted codes work and the occasional simple example to get you started. After all, you're a programmer and you don't need step-by-step instructions on using this language.

And you've got the right book in your hands. This book is not a step-by-step learning tool, but rather a reference tool for reminding yourself about how certain elements of C++ work. You can keep this book by your computer or workstation and consult the book whenever you need a quick-fix of C++ syntax.

How This Book Is Organized

This book is made of 13 parts, and the elements in the parts are organized alphabetically within each part. To find information about a program element, think about what specific element of C++ programming it falls under and then look in the appropriate part. For example, to find the naming conventions for constants, look in "Part II: Constants and Variables," check under the heading "Constants," and look for the heading "Naming conventions for constants."

This book's 13 parts are organized by subject matter, as follows:

Part I: Getting to Know C++ — Here's where I cover compiling a C++ program, using comments, and understanding the language's special characters, among other subjects.

Part II: Constants and Variables — Topics include using constants, variables, and reference variables.

Part III: Operators — Go to this part for information about the different kinds of operators (Boolean, arithmetic, and the like), as well as the details of typecasting.

Part IV: Input and Output (Streaming) — Here's all you ever wanted to know about the stream library, which is the heart and soul of input and output for C++.

Part V: Decision-Making — Good old-fashioned if-then and related statements are covered in this part. I also go into the complexities of the switch statement.

Part VI: Loops — Travel to the wonderful world of loops; visit the exciting do-while and for codes, see loops in their nests, and uncover the mysterious word *iterations*.

Part VII: Data Types, Enumerated Types, and Data Structures — Data types and structures are the topic of this part. Look here for unions as well.

Part VIII: Arrays — Dynamic, single, and multiple arrays are covered in detail. *Note:* Check out Part IX for any information on arrays and pointers.

Part IX: Pointers — I discuss all kinds of pointers here, including pointers to programming elements that are the topic of other parts. For example, you get the scoop on pointers to functions and variables in this part instead of in Part X or Part II. Look here also for the relationship between pointers and arrays.

Part X: Functions and Arguments — Glance through these pages for the dish on how C++ uses arguments and functions. You also find information about using strings as arguments.

Part XI: Strings — Nearly everything about C++ and strings appears in this part: Initializing, concatenating, and reversing strings, for example. *Note:* The topic of using strings as arguments appears in Part X instead of in this part.

Part XII: Classes — Look here to find out about constructors, destructors, operators, declaring class instances, and other related information. I cover the basics of classes in this part; really high-end material about classes appears in Part XIII.

Part XIII: Advanced OOP — Here you find the skinny on inheritance, declaring class hierarchies, and the loftier concepts of classes.

Techie Talk — Every technical reference needs a good glossary, and this book is no exception. I did my best to provide you with definitions for all the strange verbiage that C++ has to offer, and I threw in the meanings for a few general programming terms just for good measure.

Conventions Used in This Book

Individual code elements, such as variable names, appear in the text this way: myVariable. Often the code that I use as an example isn't just one or two lines, so you see something similar to the following (which is incomplete code, by the way):

```
class Rabbit
{
 public:
 double getXCoord();
 double getYCoord();
 };
```

I also use italics in code to show that certain terms are used as placeholders and aren't really code. For example, you may see:

```
class className
```

The word className, which is a placeholder for the class name of your choice, is in italics to differentiate it from the word class, which is the actual syntax for the declaration.

Finally, be aware that I use *Hungarian notation* preceding the names of many program elements. These notations denote how the element is being used in the code block. Because I use a lot of Microsoft products, I prefer that company's loose version of Hungarian notation, such as: *psz* for pointer to ASCIIZ string;

n for integer; *f* for floating-point numbers (float and double); *u* for unsigned integer; *c* for character ; *b* for Boolean; and *l* for long.

Icon Legend

I use marginal icons next to certain paragraphs throughout the various parts. When you see an icon, pay special attention to the text next to it. That text can make the difference between a good program that runs just fine and a debugging nightmare. The following explains why I say this:

Text flagged with the Tip icon is super-useful information that saves you time or clarifies syntax.

Use paragraphs marked with the Fast Track icon to save yourself some programming time.

Notice that the Warning icon has the picture of a little bomb on it. Terrible things can happen if you disregard text marked with this icon. Trust me!

Something strange lurks in the depths of C++, and this icon marks spots where I uncover such scary elements.

Occasionally I can't go into a lot of detail about a particular program element, so I include a cross-reference to the appropriate chapter in *C++ For Dummies,* 2nd Edition whenever necessary. This icon marks those references.

You find the straight dope on how to use a particular C++ element wherever you see the Syntax icon.

The Example icon marks text that illustrates the use of a C++ element.

If you're an absolute beginner to C++ programming, pick up a copy of *C++ For Dummies,* 2nd Edition by Stephen R. Davis (IDG Books Worldwide, Inc.) and peruse it at your leisure.

Part 1

Getting to Know C++

This part looks at the basic aspects of programming in C++. The text covers the general outline for writing simple C++ programs and the basic parts of a C++ program. I also discuss how to add comments and use special compiler instructions.

In this part . . .

- ✓ Discovering the basics of C++
- ✓ Creating a simple C++ program
- ✓ Using comments
- ✓ Composing compiler directives
- ✓ Uncovering programs that compile C++
- ✓ Understanding rules for naming items
- ✓ Using special characters

About C++ Basics

C++ is a general-purpose programming language that is derived from the popular C language. C++ builds on C through the addition of object-oriented programming features and some minor enhancements in areas other than object-oriented programming. Because of the language's lineage, C++ is meant to be highly compatible with C.

The main difference between C++ and C is that C++ uses classes (which you can read more about in Part XII). Using classes and objects enables C++ to become a powerful language for programming sophisticated GUI (Graphical User Interface) environments such as Windows 3.*x* and Windows 95. Classes enable C++ to use (and extend) classes, programmed by others, that contain many operations to support common window tasks.

A Simple C++ Program

The following is a simple C++ program:

```
// A Simple C++ program

#include <iostream.h>

// this is a comment
/* and so is this */
/*
 and so is this one
*/

main()
{
  // the next statement displays a greeting message
  cout << "Hello World!";

  return 0;
}
```

The first line in the program contains the following comment:

```
// A Simple C++ program
```

This type of code fragment — a line of text starting with the slash characters (//) — is called a *one-line comment*. When the compiler sees such a comment, it ignores the text that comes after the // until it reaches the end of that line. In general, programmers write comments to make the code easier to understand and to remind themselves and others of the tasks that the code performs. Professional programmers may use comments to state the date that they wrote the source code, to note the version number, to list the programmers' names, and so on.

The second line of the source code includes the following special statement, which is called a *directive:*

```
#include <iostream.h>
```

The following comments appear after the #include directive:

```
// this is a comment
/* and so is this */
/*
 and so is this one
*/
```

See the section "Comments" later in this part for more about these statements.

After the comments, the listing shows the following source code:

```
main()
{
  // the next statement displays a greeting message
  cout << "Hello World!";

  return 0;
}
```

The line main() declares the function *main.* Every program must have only one function main(). A *function* is a program component that performs some action that manipulates data. The function main() acts as the point where program execution begins. The contents of function main() vary, depending on what the program does. The function returns an integer value that represents an error state. Typically, the function main() returns the value 0.

The function has a *body* of statements that is enclosed in a pair of open and closed braces (that is, the characters { and }). These braces define a *statement block,* which, in this case, makes up the function's body.

The function main() contains a one-line comment and two statements. Every statement ends with a semicolon. The following is a summary of the statements in this listing:

✦ The first statement is an *output statement.* This statement displays information on-screen to enable the program to communicate with you. The name cout is the standard *console output object* (a fancy way for programmers to refer to the monitor), which sends characters to the screen (which is also called the output screen). The characters << represent the *output operator,* a special symbol that tells the object `cout` what to display. The characters `"Hello World!"` represent a literal text (that is, verbatim text) that appears on-screen when the program runs.

✦ The second statement is `return 0`. This statement makes the function `main()` return 0, a numeric code that tells the operating system that the program ended on a happy note. All the programs in this book have the statement `return 0` as the last statement in function `main()`.

Comments

Comments are parts of the source code that the compiler ignores. Use comments to document the source code and to explain the function of the statements. You may use comments to document the programmer's name, version number, last update, and other information that you want to include in the source code.

The following are examples of the two types of comments that are supported by C++:

```
// this is a comment
/* and so is this */
/*
 and so is this one
*/
```

The first comment is a one-line comment that uses the `//` characters. Notice that the second and third comments use the `/*` and `*/` characters to declare the beginning and end of the comments. The second comment uses the `/*` and `*/` character sets on the same line. By contrast, the last comment uses the `/*` and `*/` character sets to make a comment span multiple lines. C++ supports one-line comments that use the `//` and multiple-line comments that use the `/*` and `*/` characters.

Comments make your listings more readable and easier to update.

Compiler Directives

For a programming language to perform sophisticated tasks (especially ones that are required by the operating system, complex programs, and mission-critical applications), the source code must be able to incorporate special *directives* to the compiler. These directives guide and fine-tune the action of the compiler. The following subsections look at the directives that you are most likely to use as a novice C++ programmer.

The #define directive

The #define directive defines macros. C++ has inherited this directive from C programming for the sake of software compatibility. The general syntax for the #define directive is as follows:

```
// form 1
#define identifierName
// form 2
#define identifierName literalValue
// form 3
#define identifierName(parameterList) expression
```

The first form of the #define directive is typically used to indicate that a file has been read or to flag a certain software state. In this case, the #define directive does not need to associate a value with *identifierName*. The main point for this use is to determine whether an identifier has been defined. The following are examples of using the #define directive to define state-related identifiers:

```
#define _IOSTREAM_H_
#define _DEFINES_MINMAX_
```

The above examples define the identifiers _IOSTREAM_H_ and _DEFINES_MINMAX_. The first example may indicate, for example, that the file DATA.H has been read. The second example may flag the compiler to define (or not define) certain functions.

The second form of the #define directive defines the names of constants and associates literal values (numbers, characters, strings, and so on) with these names. The preprocessor (which automatically runs before the compiler) replaces the name of the defined identifier with its associated value. The following are examples of using the #define directive to declare constants:

```
#define MAX 100
#define ARRAY_SIZE 20
#define MINUTE_PER_HOUR 60
```

These examples define the constants MAX, ARRAY_SIZE, and MINUTE_PER_HOUR and associate the values 100, 20, and 60 with these constants, respectively.

The third form of the #define directive defines pseudo-inline functions. The #define directive can create macros with arguments. In this case, the preprocessor replaces the name of the defined identifier and its arguments with its associated expression. The following are several examples:

```
#define Square(x) ((x) * (x))
#define Reciprocal(x) (1/(x))
#define Lowercase(c) (char(tolower(c))
#define Uppercase(c) (char(toupper(c))
```

These examples define the pseudo-inline functions Square, Reciprocal, Lowercase, and Uppercase.

C++ gurus advise you to avoid using the #define directive to create pseudo-inline functions. Instead, you should use the formal inline functions. The gurus have cited problems with expanding the macro's expressions. Moreover, they argue that these pseudo-inline functions perform no type-checking (as do regular functions) on their arguments — basically anything goes! For example, you can easily pass a floating-point number as an argument when the macro expects a character.

The #error directive

The #error directive makes the compiler display a message on the standard error stream and yield a nonzero integer code when the compiler terminates. The general syntax for the #error directive is as follows:

```
#error message
```

After the compiler encounters an #error directive, it scans the remaining part of the program for other syntax errors but does not generate an object file. The following is an example of using the #error directive:

```
#if defined(DEBUG_MODE)
#error Need to turn off debug mode!
#endif
```

This code generates the error message Need to turn off debug mode! if the identifier DEBUG_MODE is currently defined.

The #if and #elif directives

The #if and #elif directives enable you to offer the compiler the choice of compiling one of multiple sets of statements, depending on tested conditions. The general syntax for the #if and #elif is as follows:

```
#if expression1
// statement set #1
[#elif expression2
// statement set #2 ]
  . . .
[#else
// statement set #N]
#endif
```

If expression1 returns true (a nonzero integer), the compiler processes the first set of statements and ignores the other statements after the #elif and #else directives. By contrast, if expression1 is false, the compiler examines the conditions of the #elif directives, starting with the first #elif directive. When the compiler finds an #elif directive whose expression returns true, it processes the statements that are associated with that directive. If the expressions of the #if and #elif are false, the compiler processes the statements after the #else clause (if one is used).

The tested expressions may evaluate to a constant and may include logical operators and the operator defined. (This operator returns true if its argument is a currently defined name.) However, you cannot use the operator sizeof, type casts, floating-point types, or enumerated types.

The #ifdef and #ifndef directives

The #ifdef and #ifndef directives determine whether an identifier is defined or is not currently defined, respectively. The general syntax for the #ifdef directive is as follows:

```
// form 1
#ifdef identifierName
// statements
#endif
// form 2
#ifdef identifierName
// statements set #1
#else
// statements set #2
#endif
```

The #ifdef directive yields true (a nonzero value) if it is currently defined and yields false (0) if it is not. If the directive returns true, the compiler processes the statements between the #ifdef and #endif directives in form1 of the directive. form2 of the syntax shows that the compiler processes the first set of statements if the #ifndef directive returns true or processes the second set of statements if the directive #ifndef returns false.

The general syntax for the #ifndef directive is as follows:

```
#ifndef identifierName
// statements
#endif
// form 2
#ifndef identifierName
// statements set #1
#else
// statements set #2
#endif
```

The #ifndef directive works in the reverse manner of the #ifdef directive.

12 Compiler Directives

The following program illustrates the #ifdef and #ifndef
directives. The statements contain the source code for the
program IFDEF1.CPP. This program uses the #ifdef and #ifndef
directives along with the #define and #undef directives. The
program defines the identifier DEBUG and uses the #ifdef
directive to display a message that lets you know whether the
DEBUG identifier is currently defined. The program then undefines
DEBUG and uses the #ifndef directive to let you know whether
the DEBUG identifier is currently undefined.

```
/*
   IFDEF1.CPP

   C++ program demonstrates the #ifdef and
    #ifndef directives
*/

#include <iostream.h>

#define DEBUG

main()
{
   cout << "Testing the #ifdef directive\n";

#ifdef DEBUG
   cout << "DEBUG is currently defined\n";
#else
   cout << "DEBUG is not currently defined\n";
#endif

#undef DEBUG

   cout << "Testing the #ifndef directive\n";

#ifndef DEBUG
   cout << "DEBUG is not currently defined\n";
#else
   cout << "DEBUG is currently defined\n";
#endif

   return 0;
}
```

The following is the output of the previous program:

```
Testing the #ifdef directive
DEBUG is currently defined
Testing the #ifndef directive
```

DEBUG is not currently defined. The IFDEF1.CPP program contains
the #ifdef and #ifndef directives that are located inside the
function main(). The program uses the #define directive to
define the identifier DEBUG. When the compiler examines the

#ifdef directive, it finds that the expression in the directive returns true. Therefore, the compiler processes the stream output statement immediately after that directive and ignores the output statement after the #else directive.

The #undef statement undefines DEBUG and causes the #ifndef directive to return true. Consequently, the compiler processes the stream output statement immediately after that directive and ignores the output statement after the #else directive.

The #include directive

The first, and perhaps most widely used, compiler directive that you may see is #include. This directive instructs the compiler to read a source-code file and treat it as though you had typed its contents where the directive appears. The general syntax for the #include directive is as follows:

```
// form 1
#include <filename>
// form 2
#include "filename"
```

The first identifier *filename* represents the name of file that is to be included. The two forms of #include vary in conducting the searches for the included file. The first form searches for the file in the special directory for included files. The second form expands the search to incorporate the current directory.

The following are examples of using the #include directive:

```
#include <iostream.h>
#include "myarray.hpp"
```

The first example includes the header file IOSTREAM.H by searching for it in the directory of included files. The second example includes the header file MYARRAY.HPP by searching for it in the directory of included files as well as in the current directory.

The #undef directive

The #undef directive counteracts the #define directive by removing the definition of an identifier. The general syntax for the #undef directive is as follows:

```
#undef identifierName
```

The following is an example of using the #undef directive:

```
#define ARRAY_SIZE 100
int nArray[ARRAY_SIZE];
#undef ARRAY_SIZE
```

This code performs the following tasks:

+ It defines the identifier ARRAY_SIZE with the #define directive.

+ It uses the identifier ARRAY_SIZE to define the number of elements of array nArray.

+ It undefines the identifier ARRAY_SIZE by using the #undef directive.

You do not need to use the directive #undef to undefine an identifier before redefining it with another #define directive. Simply use the second #define directive to redefine an identifier. The following is an example of this use:

```
// first definition of ARRAY_SIZE
#define ARRAY_SIZE 100
int nArray1[ARRAY_SIZE];
#undef ARRAY_SIZE
// second definition of ARRAY_SIZE
#define ARRAY_SIZE 10
int nArray2[ARRAY_SIZE];
```

These statements define, use, undefine, redefine, and then reuse the identifier ARRAY_SIZE. The previous code yields the same array declarations as the next one, which lacks the #undef directive:

```
// first definition of ARRAY_SIZE
#define ARRAY_SIZE 100
int nArray1[ARRAY_SIZE];
// second definition of ARRAY_SIZE
#define ARRAY_SIZE 10
int nArray2[ARRAY_SIZE];
```

The preceding example shows that you can change a *constant*. This feature (using the #define directive) can make the code hard to read and debug. Using the directive #undef may be in order.

Programs That Compile C++

To compile C++ programs, your most basic needs are a compiler and linker. The software packages that compile C++ typically use an integrated development environment (IDE) that contains the needed compiler and linker and adds a text editor, debugger, online help, and other programming tools.

The popular C++ compilers (all of which include IDE) are

+ Microsoft Visual C++

+ Borland C++ and the Borland C++ Builder

+ Watcom C++

+ Symantec C++

These compilers are available from mail-order magazines as well as many retail software outlets.

Rules for Naming Items

C++ requires you to observe the following rules when using names (which are also called *identifiers*):

+ The first character must be a letter or the underscore character.

+ Subsequent characters can be letters, digits, or the underscore character.

+ The maximum length of an identifier is 247 characters. Often a maximum number of significant characters is inherent in the identifier; this number varies depending on the compiler being used.

+ Identifiers are case-sensitive in C++. Thus the names `rate`, `RATE`, and `Rate` refer to three different identifiers.

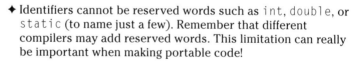

+ Identifiers cannot be reserved words such as `int`, `double`, or `static` (to name just a few). Remember that different compilers may add reserved words. This limitation can really be important when making portable code!

The following examples are of valid identifiers:

```
X
x
aString
DAYS_IN_WEEK
BinNumber0
bin_number_0
bin0Number2
_length
```

Use descriptive names that have a reasonable length. Avoid identifier names that are too short or too long. Short names yield poor readability, and long names are prone to typos.

Special Characters

C++ supports special *escape sequence* characters that start with the backslash character (\) and are followed by one or more characters. The characters \n represent the new line character that appears at the end of most output statements. The following table shows the escape sequence characters.

Sequence	Task
\a	Beep
\b	Backspace
\f	Form feed
\n	New line
\r	Carriage return
\t	Horizontal tab
\v	Vertical tab
\\	Backslash
\'	Single quote
\"	Double quote
\?	Question mark

Part II

Constants and Variables

This part looks at program components that are used by the programmer to store data. These components, *constants* and *variables,* store data that either remains fixed throughout the execution of the program or that can change during that process under certain conditions. Think of constants and variables as electronic containers of data that help you create dynamic programs.

In this part . . .

✔ **Programming with constants**

✔ **Using reference variables**

✔ **Working with variables**

Constants

C++ enables you to associate fixed values (such as numbers, characters, and strings) with names. Programmers call these names *constants*. C++ supports a special syntax for declaring a constant. In general, when you declare something in a program, you tell the C++ compiler about it. The compiler stores the declaration in a special place and looks it up later as you make reference to that information. The general syntax for declaring a constant and setting its value (in a program) is as follows:

```
const [dataType] constantName = value;
```

The declaration of a constant contains the following parts:

✦ The keyword `const` (which tells the compiler that the statement declares a constant). *Keywords* are special identifiers (that is, valid C++ names) that are reserved for special use in the C++ language.

✦ The optional data type that is associated with the constant. If you omit this part, the C++ compiler assumes that the predefined data type is `int`. Because C++ is strongly typed, associating a data type with a constant can help you write programs with fewer bugs. This feature is one of the best reasons to use a `const` instead of a #define constant.

✦ The identifier that names the constant.

✦ The value that becomes associated with the constant's name.

The value that is associated with the constant must be compatible with the data type associated with the constant. For example, you cannot declare a `double`-type constant and associate a character with that constant. Instead, you must associate a floating-point number (such as 23.45) with a `double`-type constant.

Using `const` (which has a data type associated with it) instead of a #define constant enables C++ to track the data type when using the `const`, thus enabling the compiler to flag potential errors.

The following are examples of declaring constants:

```
const MAX_DAYS = 7;
const int MINUTES_IN_HOUR = 60;
const double MY_WEIGHT_AT_BIRTH = 10;
const char HELP = '!'
```

A description of each statement is as follows:

+ The constant `MAX_DAYS`, which represents the number of days in a week, has no explicit data type associated with it. Therefore, the C++ compiler assigns the default `int` data type to that constant. The declaration of the constant `MAX_DAYS` associates the value of 7 to that constant.

+ The constant `MINUTES_IN_HOUR`, which represents the number of minutes in an hour, has the data type `int` associated with it, and the value is 60.

+ The constant `MY_WEIGHT_AT_BIRTH`, which represents my weight in pounds at birth, has the `double` type associated with it. The declaration assigns the value 10 to the constant. (Yes, I was a chunky baby!) See "Floating point data types" in Part VII for more about types.

+ The constant `HELP`, which represents a help character, has the data type `char` associated with it. Declaring the constant `HELP` associates the exclamation character (!) with it.

Naming conventions for constants

A popular way to name constants so that they're easily identifiable is to use uppercase characters and the underscore character. Examples include `MAX_ATTEMPTS`, `MIN_VALUE`, and `MAX_CLIENTS_PER_DAY`. Remember that the C++ compiler *does not* enforce this style and enables you to declare constants such as `MaxAttempts`, `minValue`, and `max_clients_per_day`. But to have the look of a professional programmer, you should retain the use of uppercase characters.

Using constants

The following program declares and displays the values of constants. The program shows you how the declaration of various kinds of constants (having the data types `int`, `double`, and `char`) appears in a program. The program also displays the values that are associated with these constants to confirm the association between the names of the constants and their values.

The following shows the source code for the program CONST.CPP:

```
/* CONST.CPP
 A C++ program that illustrates declaring and
 constants and displaying their values
*/
#include <iostream.h>
```

(continued)

(continued)

```
main()
{
  // declare an int-type constant
  const int MAX_DAYS = 7;
  // declare a double-type constant
  const double DAYS_IN_YEAR = 365.25;
  // declare char-type constants
  const char PROMPT = '>';
  const char NEW_LINE = '\n';

  // display the value of constant MAX_DAYS
  cout << "There are " << MAX_DAYS
       << " days in a week" << NEW_LINE;
  // display the value of constant DAYS_IN_YEAR
  cout << "The are actually " << DAYS_IN_YEAR
       << " days in a year" << NEW_LINE;
  // display the value of constant PROMPT
  cout << "The prompt character is " << PROMPT
       << NEW_LINE;
  return 0;
}
```

This code generates the following output:

```
There are 7 days in a week
There are actually 365.25 days in a year
The prompt character is >
```

The previous program declares the following constants:

+ Constant MAX_DAYS has the data type int and the value 7.

+ Constant DAYS_IN_YEAR has the data type double and the
  value 365.25. This constant represents the actual number of
  days in a year.

+ Constant PROMPT has the data type char and the value of >.
  This constant represents a prompt character.

+ Constant NEW_LINE has the data type char and the value \n.
  The program uses this constant to send a new line to the
  output screen.

The program uses three output statements to write the values of
the constants MAX_DAYS, DAYS_IN_YEAR, and PROMPT to the
screen. The output statements use the constant NEW_LINE to send
a new line to the screen. Each output statement includes a *string
literal* (that is, text that appears in quotation marks) that clarifies
the value of the constant in that statement.

Using type definitions

You often use data types in a programming language, especially the basic predefined ones, in different contexts. For example, the int type serves as an array index, a counter for a number of items, pixel coordinates, and even logical values, to name a few. C++ enables you to create alias types that make your source code easier to read and understand. The typedef statement creates the data type aliases and has the following syntax:

```
typedef oldType newType;
```

The oldType parameter represents a previously defined type (either a predefined data type or a user-data type). The newType parameter represents the new alias. The following are examples using the typedef statement:

```
// Example 1
typedef int Logical;
// Example 2
typedef int ArrayIndexType;
// Example 3
typedef int NumberOfElemsType;
// Example 4
typedef double WeightType;
// Example 5
typedef double SalaryType;
// Example 6
typedef double AreaType;
```

Example 1 uses the typedef statement to create the Logical type as an alias type for int. Using the Logical type identifier is clearer than int for variables and parameters that store logical data. For example, the following prototype of function show1 is a bit easier to read than function show2:

```
void show1(Logical bDisplayInOneLine);
void show2(int bDisplayInOneLine);
```

Example 2 uses the typedef statement to create the type ArrayIndexType as an alias for int. Again, using the ArrayIndexType is clearer than int for variables and parameters that represent array indices.

Example 3 uses the typedef statement to create the type NumberOfElemsType as an alias for int. Once more, using the NumberOfElemsType is clearer than int for variables and parameters that represent numbers of elements in an array.

Similarly, examples 4, 5, and 6 use the typedef statement to create the types WeightType, SalaryType, and AreaType as aliases to the predefined type double. Using these alias types brings a clearer meaning to their related variables and parameters.

C++ enables you to create aliases for single-dimensional and multidimensional arrays. The general syntax for this kind of alias type is as follows:

```
typedef basicElemType
    sdArrayType[numberOfElements];
typedef basicElemType
    mdArrayType[Elems1][Elems2]...;
```

The `typedef` statement creates a single-array type by stating the type of the basic element of the array, the array name, and the number of elements. In the case of a multidimensional array, the `typedef` statement lists the size of each dimension.

The following are examples creating array type aliases:

```
// Example 1
typedef int weekDays[7];
// Example 2
const int MAX_ROWS = 25;
const int MAX_COLS = 80;
typedef char textScreen[MAX_ROWS][MAX_COLS];
```

Example 1 defines the alias array type `weekDays` as an `int`-type array of 7 elements. The second example defines the alias matrix type `textScreen` as a `char`-type matrix of `MAX_ROWS` and `MAX_COLS`.

Defining variables and parameters by using the alias array type merely requires using the name of the alias array type. You must not include the number of array elements. The following examples use the alias types `weekDays` and `textScreen`:

```
main()
{
    weekDays theDays; // array of 7 in-type elements
    textScreen theScreen // matrix of characters
    // other statements
}
```

Reference Variables

Reference variables are aliases to existing variables and do not have their own storage allocated. C++ requires that the declaration of a reference variable includes its initialization. It is important to understand that the initial value of a reference variable is permanent. You cannot change the reference variable to be an alias for a different variable. The general syntax for declaring a reference variable is as follows:

```
type& refVar = referencedVariable;
```

You can use a reference variable to access the value of the referenced variable. The following is an example of declaring and using a reference variable:

```
int nNum = 10;
int& rNum = nNum;

cout << rNum << "\n"; // displays 10
rNum++; // nNum is now 11
cout << nNum << "\n"; // displays 11
```

This example declares and initializes the `int`-type variable `nNum`. The example also declares the reference variable `rNum` and initializes it by using the variable `nNum`. The first output statement displays the value of variable `nNum` by using the reference variable `rNum`. This example applies the increment operator to the reference variable `rNum`; this operator increments the value in the variable `nNum`. The second output statement displays the new value in variable `nNum` (which is now 11).

Reference variables are more useful with class instances than with variables of predefined types. You can use a reference to a class together with typecasting to access the data of an object in a particular way. This usage of reference variables is very advanced and is beyond the scope of this book. (I mention this so that you know that reference variables are not a waste.)

For a broader discussion of reference variables, *see* Chapter 4 of *C++ For Dummies,* 2nd Edition.

Variables

A *variable* is a name that can store a value. You can change the value that is associated with the variable when the program runs. C++ supports a special syntax for declaring a variable. The general syntax for declaring a variable is as follows:

```
dataType variableName [= value];
```

The declaration of a variable contains the following parts:

✦ The data type that is associated with the variable

✦ The identifier that names the variable

✦ The optional value that assigns an initial value to the variable

A variable that is not initialized has garbage as data and corrupts your code!

You can declare multiple variables (that have the same type) in the same statement. The general syntax for this kind of declaration is as follows:

```
dataType var1 [= value1], var2 [= value2], …;
```

Examples of declaring variables include the following:

```
int NumberOfDisks;
long FileSize;
char MiddleInitial;
int Index, Count, DayNum = 1;
double InterestRate = 0.045;
```

A brief description of each statement is as follows:

◆ The first example declares the variable NumberOfDisks as an int-type variable. Therefore, the variable NumberOfDisks can store values that are defined by the int type. For example, the variable NumberOfDisks can store the integer 10. The declaration of variable NumberOfDisks does not initialize (that is, assign an *initial* value in the declaration to) that variable with a value.

◆ The second example declares the variable FileSize as a long-type variable. Therefore, the variable FileSize can store values that are defined by the long type. For example, the variable FileSize can store the integer value of 500,000. The declaration of the variable FileSize does not initialize that variable with a value. See the table under "Integer data types" in Part VII, "Data Types, Enumerated Types, and Data Structures," for more about types.

◆ The third example declares the variable MiddleInitial as a char-type variable. This variable can store any character, such as *A, H,* or *K.* The declaration of variable MiddleInitial does not initialize that variable with a value.

◆ The fourth example declares the three int-type variables, namely, Index, Count, and DayNum. The declaration initializes the variable DayNum with the value of 1. These variables store integers such as –5, 4, and 345.

◆ The last example declares the variable InterestRate as a double-type variable. The declaration also initializes this variable with the value of 0.045 (the decimal equivalent of 4.5 percent).

The following programming example shows these features:

◆ Declaring variables of different data types

◆ Assigning values to the variables

◆ Displaying the values in the variables

◆ Assigning new values to the variables

◆ Displaying the new values in the variables

The program, VAR1.CPP, is as follows:

```
/* VAR1.CPP
 A C++ program that shows how to declare
 and use variables
*/
#include <iostream.h>
main()
{
 // declare a char-type variable
 char Letter;
 // declare a double-type variable
 double Number;
 // declare and int-type variable
 int Integer;
 // assign character to variable Letter
 Letter = 'X';
 // display character in variable Letter
 cout << "Variable Letter stores " << Letter <<
    "\n";
 // assign another character to variable Letter
 Letter = 'A';
 // display new character in variable Letter
 cout << "Variable Letter now stores "
    << Letter << "\n";
 // assign number to variable Number
 Number = 251.65;
 // display value in variable Number
 cout << "Variable Number stores " << Number <<
    "\n";
 // assign a new number to variable Number
 Number = -543.32;
 // display new value in variable Number
 cout << "Variable Number now stores " << Number
    << "\n";
 // assign number to variable Integer
 Integer = 1234;
 // display value in variable Integer
 cout << "Variable Integer stores " << Integer <<
    "\n";
 // assign a new number to variable Integer
 Integer = -32001;
 // display new value in variable Integer
 cout << "Variable Integer now stores " << Integer
    << "\n";
 return 0;
}
```

This program generates the following output:

```
Variable Letter stores X
Variable Letter now stores A
Variable Number stores 251.65
Variable Number now stores -543.32
Variable Integer stores 1234
Variable Integer now stores -32001
```

The program declares the following variables:

+ The char-type variable Letter, which stores characters

+ The double-type variable Number, which stores double-precision, floating-point numbers

+ The int-type variable Integer, which stores integers

Notice that the declarations of the preceding variables do not initialize these variables with values.

The function main() performs the following tasks:

+ Stores the letter *X* in the variable Letter.

+ Displays the character stored in the variable Letter by using an output statement (which displays the character *X*).

+ Stores the letter *A* in the variable Letter. Notice that the compiler is not affected when you assign a new value to a variable. Remember, a variable is simply a placeholder for data that can change.

+ Displays the character stored in the variable Letter by using an output statement (which displays the character *A*).

+ Stores the number 251.65 in the variable Number.

+ Displays the number stored in variable Number by using an output statement (which displays the value 251.65).

+ Stores a new number, –543.32, in the variable Number.

+ Displays the new number stored in the variable Number by using an output statement (which displays the value –543.32).

+ Stores the integer 1234 in the variable Integer.

+ Displays the number stored in the variable Integer by using an output statement (which displays the value 1234).

+ Stores a new integer, –32001, in the variable Integer.

+ Displays the new number stored in the variable Integer by using an output statement (which displays the value –32001).

Part III

Operators

This part covers *operators,* which are program parts that you use to manipulate and query data. Without operators, data would simply sit idle in programs and computers would become totally useless! This part looks at the various kinds of operators. Some operators work with numbers, others with logical values, and still others work on the bits in data.

In this part . . .

✔ **Adding up arithmetic operators**

✔ **Working with assignment operators**

✔ **Using Boolean and relational operators**

✔ **Understanding bit manipulation operators**

✔ **Using the comma operator**

✔ **Working with decrement and increment operators**

✔ **Understanding dynamic allocation operators**

✔ **Working with pointer operators**

✔ **Using the** sizeof **operator**

✔ **Discovering typecasting**

Arithmetic Operators

Most of the C++ operators work with *numerical* data types that include integer types (such as int, long, and unsigned) and floating-point types (such as float and double). The *modulus* operator (using the symbol %), however, works with integer types only. This operator returns the remainder of the division between two integers. The arithmetic operators require two numerical items, called *operands*. The following table lists the arithmetic operators in C++.

C++ Operator	Role	Data Type	Example
+	Plus sign (the plus sign in front of a number or variable)	Numerical	z = +h - 2
-	Minus sign (the minus sign in front of a number or variable)	Numerical	z = -1 * (z+1)
+	Add	Numerical	h = 34 + g
-	Subtract	Numerical	z = 3.4 - t
/	Divide	Numerical	d = m / v
*	Multiply	Numerical	area = len * wd
%	Modulus	Integer	count = w % 12

In addition to the obvious division-by-zero error, the operators +, -, *, and / run the risk of generating results outside the valid range of the data types that are involved with these operations. To solve this problem, use (and assign the results to) data types that have a wider range of values than the operands (that is, numbers, variables, constants, and so on) that are used with the operators.

Assignment Operators

C++ supports the mathematical assignment operators that combine the effect of using the *assignment operator* (the = sign) and any of the arithmetic operators (such as - and +). In other words, a mathematical assignment operator is a shorthand form of using the assignment operator and one of the arithmetic operators. The following table lists the arithmetic assignment operators that are used in C++. The table also contains examples of using these operators in addition to the long-form versions (that is, the ones that use the assignment operator and an arithmetic operator) of the statements.

C++ Operator	Example	Long-Form Example
+=	fSum += fX;	fSum = fSum + fX;
-=	fY -= fX;	fY = fY - fX;
/=	nCount /= N;	nCount = nCount / N;
*=	fScl *= fFactor;	fScl = fScl * fFactor;
%=	nBins %= nCount;	nBins = nBins % nCount;

The following points discuss what the examples in the previous table accomplish:

✦ The first example uses the operator += to add the value in variable fX to that in variable fSum.

✦ The second example uses the operator -= to subtract the value in variable fX from the value in variable fY.

✦ The third example uses the operator /= to divide the value in variable nCount by the value in variable N.

✦ The fourth example uses the operator *= to multiply the value in variable fScl by the value in variable fFactor.

✦ The last example uses the operator %= to store in variable nBins the remainder of dividing the value in variable nBins by the value in variable nCount.

Boolean and Relational Operators

Programs require relational and Boolean operators to create decision-making Boolean expressions. The following table shows the relational and Boolean operators that are used in C++. Notice that the list lacks the logical operator XOR. However, the table contains the conditional assignment operator ? :. This operator is probably new to you (unless you program in C) and has the following syntax:

```
(expression) ? trueValue : falseValue
```

The operator yields the trueValue if the expression is true (or nonzero) and returns the falseValue otherwise. Therefore, use the conditional assignment operator to assign a value to a variable, as shown here:

```
variable = (expression) ? trueValue : falseValue;
```

This statement is similar to the following if statement:

```
if (expression)
 variable = trueValue;
else
 variable = falseValue;
```

C++ Operator	Meaning	Example
&&	Logical AND	k > 1 && k < 11
||	Logical OR	k < 0 || k > 22
!	Logical NOT	!(k > 1 && k < 10)
<	Less than	k < 12
<=	Less than or equal to	k <= 33
>	Greater than	k > 45
>=	Greater than or equal to	k >= 77
==	Equal to	k == 32
!=	Not equal to	k != 33
?:	Conditional assignment	k = (k < 0)? 1 : k

I now present a programming example that uses the relational and Boolean operators. The following source code is for the program RELOP1.CPP, which generates three random numbers in the range of 1 to 100. The program then tests the following conditions:

+ The first number is less than the second number.

+ The first number is less than or equal to the third number.

+ The second number is greater than the third number.

+ The first and second numbers are equal.

+ The first and third numbers are not equal.

+ The first number is less than the second number, and the second number is less than the third number.

+ The first number is less than the second number, or the second number is less than the third number.

+ The first number is not less than and not equal to the second number.

The program displays each test and the outcome of that test.

```
// C++ program demonstrates relational
// and Boolean operators

#include <iostream.h>
#include <stdlib.h>
#include <time.h>

main()
{
  const int LO = 1;
  const int HI = 100;

  int nNum1, nNum2, nNum3;
```

```
// reseed the random number generator using the
   system time
srand((unsigned)time(NULL));
// get the three random numbers
nNum1 = rand() % HI + LO;
nNum2 = rand() % HI + LO;
nNum3 = rand() % HI + LO;

cout << "First number is " << nNum1 << "\n"
   << "Second number is " << nNum2 << "\n"
   << "Third number is " << nNum3 << "\n";

cout << nNum1 << " < " << nNum2 << " is "
   << ((nNum1 < nNum2) ? "TRUE" : "FALSE") <<
   "\n";
cout << nNum1 << " <= " << nNum3 << " is "
   << ((nNum1 <= nNum3) ? "TRUE" : "FALSE") <<
   "\n";
cout << nNum2 << " > " << nNum3 << " is "
   << ((nNum2 > nNum3) ? "TRUE" : "FALSE") <<
   "\n";
cout << nNum1 << " == " << nNum2 << " is "
   << ((nNum1 == nNum2) ? "TRUE" : "FALSE") <<
   "\n";
cout << nNum1 << " != " << nNum3 << " is "
   << ((nNum1 != nNum3) ? "TRUE" : "FALSE") <<
   "\n";

cout << nNum1 << " < " << nNum2 << " AND "
   << nNum2 << " < " << nNum3 << " is "
   << ((nNum1 < nNum2 && nNum2 < nNum3) ? "TRUE" :
   "FALSE")
   << "\n";
cout << nNum1 << " < " << nNum2 << " OR "
   << nNum2 << " < " << nNum3 << " is "
   << ((nNum1 < nNum2 || nNum2 < nNum3) ? "TRUE" :
   "FALSE")
   << "\n";
cout << "NOT (" << nNum1 << " <= " << nNum2 << " )
   is "
   << ((!(nNum1 <= nNum2)) ? "TRUE" : "FALSE")
   << "\n";

return 0;
}
```

The following is a sample output of the preceding program.
(Remember, because this program generates random numbers,
you should very rarely get the output that is shown here.)

```
First number is 41
Second number is 65
Third number is 29
41 < 65 is TRUE
41 <= 29 is FALSE
```

(continued)

(continued)

```
65 > 29 is TRUE
41 == 65 is FALSE
41 != 29 is TRUE
41 < 65 AND 65 < 29 is FALSE
41 < 65 OR 65 < 29 is TRUE
NOT (41 <= 65 ) is FALSE
```

The function `main()`, in the program RELOP1.CPP, declares the `int`-type constants `LO` and `HI`, which define the range of random numbers to generate. The function also declares the three `int`-type variables `nNum1`, `nNum2`, and `nNum3`. The function calls function `srand()` to seed the random number generator. The function `main()` then assigns three random numbers to the variables `nNum1`, `nNum2`, and `nNum3`. The function `rand()` generates the random number and, together with the constants `LO` and `HI`, provides the program with the desired range of random numbers.

The function `main()` uses a set of stream output statements to display the test for the relational and Boolean operators and to display the results of the test. Notice that the output statements use the conditional operator to invoke the relational and Boolean operators. In each statement, the conditional operator yields the string `TRUE` or `FALSE` if the tested condition is true or false, respectively. The function `main()` uses the following expressions in the relational and Boolean operators:

◆ The expression `nNum1 < nNum2` determines whether the first number is less than the second number.

◆ The expression `nNum1 <= nNum3` determines whether the first number is less than or equal to the third number.

◆ The expression `nNum2 > nNum3` determines whether the second number is greater than the third number.

◆ The expression `nNum1 == nNum2` determines whether the first and second numbers are equal.

◆ The expression `nNum1 != nNum3` determines whether the first and third numbers are not equal.

◆ The expression `nNum1 < nNum2 && nNum2 < nNum3` determines whether the first number is less than the second number and the second number is less than the third number.

◆ The expression `nNum1 < nNum2 || nNum2 < nNum3` determines whether the first number is less than the second number or whether the second number is less than the third number.

◆ The expression `!(nNum1 <= nNum2)` determines whether the first number is not less than and not equal to the second number.

Bit Manipulation Operators

C++ supports system programming (which requires bit manipulation). The following table shows the bit-manipulation operators that are used in C++. Notice that C++ supports the bitwise AND, OR, XOR, and NOT operators.

C++ Operator	Meaning	Example
&	Bitwise AND	m & 255
|	Bitwise OR	k | 122
^	Bitwise XOR	i ^ 44
~	Bitwise NOT	~k
<<	Bitwise shift left	m << 3
>>	Bitwise shift right	m >> 4

The following table contains the bit-manipulation assignment operators that are used in C++.

C++ Operator	Example	Long Form
&=	n &= 23	n = n & 23
|=	k |= 122	k = k | 122
^=	i ^= 44	i = i ^ 44
<<=	m <<= 3	m = m << 3
>>=	m >>= 4	m = m >> 4

The Comma Operator

The comma operator enables the evaluation of multiple expressions in a statement. A typical example of using the comma operator is in a `for` loop, which has multiple loop control variables. The following is an example:

```
for(int = 0, j = MAX - 1; i < j; i++, j--)
```

This `for` loop declares the variables i and j to control the loop's iterations. The initialization statement uses the comma operator to initialize both loop control variables in the same statement. Likewise, the increment part of the loop increments variable i and decrements variable j. The comma operator separates the two expressions in the increment part.

Decrement and Increment Operators

C++ offers the increment and decrement operators ++ and -- to support a shorthand syntax for adding or subtracting 1 from the value in a variable, respectively. The general syntax for the operator ++ is as follows:

```
// form 1: pre-increment
++variableName
// form 2: post-increment
variableName++
```

The pre-increment version of the operator ++ increments the value in its operand *variableName before* that variable supplies its value to the host expression. By contrast, the post-increment version of the operator ++ increments the value in its operand *variableName after* that variable supplies its value to the host expression. If you use the increment operator in a statement that has no other operators (including the assignment operator), it makes no difference which form of the operator you use. Therefore, the following two statements have the same effect:

```
nCount++;
++nCount;
```

The following are examples of using the increment operator:

```
int nCount = 1;
int nNum;
nNum = nCount++; // nNum stores 1 and nCount stores
2
nNum = ++nCount; // nNum stores 3 and nCount stores
3
```

In this code, the variable nCount has the initial value of 1. The first statement that uses the increment operator uses the post-increment version. Consequently, the statement assigns the value in variable nCount to the variable nNum and then increments the value in the variable nCount. The result is that variable nNum stores 1 and variable nCount contains 2. The second statement that uses the increment operator uses the pre-increment version. Consequently, the statement first increments the value in variable nCount and then assigns the value in variable nCount to the variable nNum. The result is that both variables nNum and nCount store 3.

The general syntax for the decrement operator is as follows:

```
// form 1: pre-decrement
--variableName
// form 2: post-decrement
variableName--
```

The pre-decrement version of the operator -- decrements the value in its operand *variableName* *before* that variable supplies its value to the host expression. By contrast, the post-decrement version of the operator -- decrements the value in its operand *variableName* *after* that variable supplies its value to the host expression. If you use the decrement operator in a statement that has no other operators (including the assignment operator), it makes no difference which form of the operator you use. Therefore, the following two statements have the same effect:

```
nCount--;
--nCount;
```

The following are examples of using the decrement operator:

```
int nCount = 10;
int nNum;
nNum = nCount--; // nNum stores 10 and nCount
    stores 9
nNum = --nCount; // nNum stores 8 and nCount
    stores 8
```

In this code, the variable nCount has the initial value of 10. The first statement that uses the decrement operator uses the post-decrement version. Consequently, the statement assigns the value in variable nCount to the variable nNum and then decrements the value in variable nCount. The result is that variable nNum stores 10 and variable nCount contains 9. The second statement that uses the decrement operator uses the pre-decrement version. Consequently, the statement first decrements the value in variable nCount and then assigns the value in variable nCount to the variable nNum. The result is that both variables nNum and nCount store 8.

Dynamic Allocation Operators

When you declare a variable in a program, the compiler prepares memory space for that variable. This preparation enables the C++ program to create this memory space when it starts to run. C++ enables you to create (and remove) additional variables when the program is running. Programmers call this kind of variable a *dynamic variable*. Dynamic variables reside in the dynamic memory area. Because you create dynamic variables at runtime, these variables do not have names associated with them, as do ordinary variables. Thus C++ uses pointers to create, access, and remove dynamic variables.

At any give time, a dynamic variable or array must have at least one pointer associated with that variable or array. If the pointer to the dynamic variable or array points somewhere else, the program loses access to the information in that variable or array.

C++ offers the operators new and delete to create and remove dynamic variables (including simple variables, structures, and objects) and arrays during program execution.

The operator new

The operator new creates dynamic variables and arrays that must always be accessed by a pointer. You can have more than one pointer accessing a dynamic variable or array. You can also switch from one pointer to another.

The general syntax for creating a new dynamic variable is as follows:

```
pointerToVar = new dataType;
```

The general syntax requires you to specify the data type that is compatible with the pointer and to assign the address of the dynamic variable to a compatible pointer. If you create a dynamic object or array of objects, the runtime system automatically invokes the constructor of the class associated with these objects.

The following are examples of creating dynamic variables:

```
struct myData {
...
};

class myClass {
...
};

int* pInt; // pointer to an int
myData* pData; // pointer to a myData structure
myClass* pClass; // pointer to class myClass
pInt = new int; // create an int-type dynamic
    variable
pmyData = new myData; // create a myData-type
    dynamic structure
pmyClass = new myClass; // create a dynamic
    instance of class myClass
```

This example declares the structure myData and the class myClass. The example also declares three pointers: the int-type pointer pInt, the myData-type pointer pmyData, and the myClass-type pointer pmyClass. The code contains statements that allocate the following dynamic variables by using the operator new:

+ An int-type dynamic variable. This task assigns the address of the dynamic variable to the pointer pInt.

+ A myData-type dynamic structure. This task assigns the address of the dynamic structure to the pointer pmyData.

✦ A myClass-type dynamic object. This task assigns the address of the dynamic object to the pointer pmyClass.

The general syntax for creating a new dynamic array is as follows:

```
pointerToArray = new dataType[numberOfElements];
```

This syntax requires you to specify the data type of the dynamic array and the number of array elements and assigns the address of the dynamic array to a compatible pointer. That pointer stores the address of the first element in the dynamic array.

The following is an example of creating a dynamic array:

```
int* pIntArr; // pointer to an int
pIntArr = new int[10]; // create an int-type
   dynamic array
```

This example declares the int-type pointer pIntArr and then creates a dynamic array of int-type elements. The example uses the operator new to create an array with 10 elements and stores the address of the dynamic array in the pointer pIntArr.

The operator delete

The operator delete removes the dynamic variables and arrays that you created with the operator new. Thus the operator delete enables you to free dynamic memory for reuse. C++ does not support automatic garbage collection, a feature that has the runtime remove dynamic variables and arrays whenever they reach the end of their scope.

Because C++ does not have automatic garbage collection, you must remove dynamic variables, arrays, and so on by using the delete operator. If you do not remove unneeded dynamic variables, you risk running out of dynamic memory space!

The general syntax for using the operator delete is as follows:

```
delete pointerToVar;
delete [] pointerToArray;
```

This syntax shows that you delete a dynamic variable by using a pointer that accesses that variable or array. In the case of an array, you need brackets ([]) to notify the compiler that you are deleting a dynamic array.

The following are examples of deleting a dynamic variable and a dynamic array:

```
delete pInt;
delete [] pIntArr;
```

The first statement deletes the dynamic variable that is accessed by the pointer pInt. The second statement removes the dynamic array that is accessed by the pointer pIntArr.

Pointer Operators

C++ offers operators that you can use to work with pointers. The following table shows these operators.

C++ Operator	Meaning	Example
&	Address-of	pInt = &myIntVar
*	Indirection (access)	cout << *pInt;
->	Indirection (select a member)	struct Point {int mX; in mY;
};	Point* pData = new Point;	pData->mX = 10;

Note: pData->mX is shorthand for (*pData).mX.

Sizeof Operator

C++ offers the operator sizeof to return the byte size of a data type or a variable. The general syntax for using the operator sizeof is as follows:

```
// form 1:
sizeof(dataType)
// form 2
sizeof(variableName)
```

The following are examples using the sizeof operator:

```
char cDriveName;
int nCharSize = sizeof(char);
int nDriveNameSize = sizeof(cDriveName);
```

This code declares the char-type variable cDriveName and the int-type variables nCharSize and nDriveNameSize. The declaration of variable nCharSize initializes this variable by using the result of the expression sizeof(char). The declaration of variable nDriveNameSize initializes this variable by using the result of the expression sizeof(nDriveNameSize).

Typecasting

Most popular programming language compilers perform automatic data type conversions (on standard types only), especially in mathematical and Boolean expressions. The compiler often promotes an integer type into a floating-point type. C++ is no exception. Moreover, C++ supports the typecasting feature to enable you to explicitly convert a value from one data type into another type. The general syntax for typecasting is as follows:

```
// form 1
(newType)expression
// form 2
newType(expression)
```

The following are examples using the typecasting feature:

```
char cLetter = 'A'
int nASCII = int(cLetter);
long lASCII = (long)cLetter;
```

This code declares and initializes the char-type variable cLetter. The code also declares the int-type variable nASCII and initializes it by using the int typecast of the variable cLetter. In addition, the code declares the long-type variable lASCII and initializes it by using the long typecast of the variable cLetter.

Input and Output (Streaming)

C++ has no built-in operators to support input and output (I/O). Instead, C++ relies on libraries for input/output that is related to the console, file, and other devices. C++ uses the metaphor of *streams* to manage the flow of data. You can regard the flow of data to and from devices such as the screen, keyboard, and files as similar to the process of using a magnetic tape cassette or cartridge. For some devices, such as files, you can control the flow of data in a manner similar to fast-forwarding, rewinding, playing, and recording on the magnetic cassette tape. For other devices, say, the screen and keyboard, you pretty much deal with an irreversible flow of data.

In this part . . .

- ✔ Performing basic stream input/output
- ✔ Handling common file stream I/O functions
- ✔ Working with random-access stream I/O
- ✔ Carrying out sequential binary stream I/O
- ✔ Performing sequential text stream I/O
- ✔ Using the stream library

Basic Stream Input/Output

C++ relies on libraries for input/output that is related to console, file, and other devices. The stream library provides the operators << and >> for output and input, respectively. To use the stream library for console I/O, you must include the file IOSTREAM.H in your source code. This header file makes the standard console output object cout available. This object works with the output operator <<. The following are examples of using the object cout and the operator <<:

```
cout << 12.34;
cout << 1 << ' ' << 2 << ' ' << 3;
```

The first example displays the number 12.34 on the output console (such as an MS-DOS screen). The second example displays the output 1 2 3, which combines integers and characters. You can mix output to include any value in the predefined types (as well as string literals).

The stream library offers the standard input stream object cin and the operator >> to support keyboard input. This object supports input to predefined data types. The following is an example:

```
int aNum;
cout << "Enter a number : ";
cin >> aNum;
cout << "You entered " << aNum;
```

This code declares the int-type variable aNum. Then the code displays a prompt message by using the object cout. The third statement takes the keyboard input (using the object cin and operator >>) and stores it in the variable aNum. The last statement uses the object cout to display the number in the variable aNum.

Common File Stream I/O Functions

The C++ stream library offers a set of member functions that are common to all file stream I/O operations. This section presents these member functions.

Close member function

The member function close() flushes any awaiting output and closes the file stream buffer. The declaration for this member function is as follows:

```
void close( );
```

The following example uses the member function `close()`:

```
char cAutoExec = "\\AUTOEXEC.BAT";
fstream f;
// open for input
f.open(cAutoExec, ios::in);
// I/O statements
f.close(); // close file stream buffer
```

This example opens the file AUTOEXEC.BAT for input, performs input operations (not shown in the code), and then closes the file stream buffer.

Open member function

The member function `open()`, as the name suggests, opens the file stream for input, output, append, and both input and output. The member function enables you to specify whether the file stream I/O is in text or binary mode. The declaration of the member function `open()` is as follows:

```
void open(const char* szName, int nMode,
 int nProt = filebuf::openprot);
```

The parameter `szName` is the name of the file to open. The parameter `nMode` is an integer that contains the mode bits defined as `ios` enumerators that can be combined with the bitwise OR operator (`|`). A table later in this part shows these enumerators. The parameter `nProt` is the file protection specification. This parameter has a default argument of `filebuf::openprot`, which is the default file protection.

The following examples use the member function `open`:

```
// example 1
char cAutoExec = "\\AUTOEXEC.BAT";
fstream f;
// open for input
f.open(cAutoExec, ios::in);

// example 2
fstream f;
// open for output
f.open("MYDATA.DAT", ios::out);

// example 3
fstream f;
// open for random access I/O
f.open("RECORDS.DAT", ios::in | ios::out |
    ios::binary);
```

The first example opens the file AUTOEXEC.BAT for text input. The second example opens the file MYDATA.DAT for text output. The last example opens the file RECORDS.DAT for binary input and output (which is really random-access mode).

Other member functions

In addition to the member functions open() and close(), the C++ stream library offers the following member functions and operators inherited from class ios:

✦ The member function good() returns a nonzero value if no error is in a stream operation. The declaration of this member function is as follows:

```
int good();
```

✦ The member function fail() returns a nonzero value if an error is in a stream operation. The declaration of this member function is as follows:

```
int fail();
```

✦ The member function eof() returns a nonzero value if the stream has not reached the end of the file. The declaration of this member function is as follows:

```
int eof();
```

✦ The overloaded operator ! determines the error status. This operator takes on a stream object as an argument.

Random-Access Stream I/O

Random-access file stream uses the member functions write(), read(), and seekg(). The latter member function enables you to move the stream pointer to the location of the next input or output. The declaration of member function seekg() in class istream is as follows:

```
istream& seekg(streampos pos);
istream& seekg(streamoff off, ios::seek_dir dir);
```

The parameter pos is the new position value (the type streampos is defined as, or has a typedef of, long). The parameter off specifies the new offset value (the type streamoff is a typedef equivalent to the predefined type long). The parameter dir specifies the seek direction and must be one of the following enumerators:

◆ The enumerator `ios::beg`, which seeks from the beginning of the stream

◆ The enumerator `ios::cur`, which seeks from the current position in the stream

◆ The enumerator `ios::end`, which seeks from the end of the stream

The following example uses the member function `seekg()`:

```
const int MAX_CHARS = 80;
char cName[MAX_CHARS + 1] = "Namir Shammas";
int nRecordNumber = 2;
int nNumChars = strlen(cName) + 1;
fstream f;
f.open("MYDATA.DAT:, ios::out | ios:in |
    ios::binary);
// seek a specific record
f.seekg(nRecordNumber * MAX_CHARS);
// read the characters
f.read((const unsigned char*)cName, MAX_CHARS);
f.close();
```

This example opens the file MYDATA.DAT for binary input and output by sending the C++ message `open()` to the object f (an instance of class `fstream`). The example sets the stream pointer to read record number `nRecordNumber`. The argument for the `seekg()` message is the expression `nRecordNumber * MAX_CHARS`. Here, constant `MAX_CHARS` represents the length of a record that stores a single string.

Sequential Binary Stream I/O

The C++ stream library offers the member functions `read()` and `write()` to read from and write to file streams.

Write member function

The class `ostream` declares the member function `write()` as follows:

```
ostream& write(const char* pch, int nCount);
ostream& write(const unsigned char* puch, int
    nCount);
ostream& write(const signed char* psch, int
    nCount);
```

The parameters `pch`, `puch`, and `psch` are pointers to a character array. The parameter `nCount` specifies the number of characters to be written. The member function inserts the specified number of bytes from the array parameter (which acts as a memory buffer) into the stream. If the underlying file were opened in text mode, additional carriage return characters can be inserted. The member function `write()` works mainly for binary stream output. For text output, use the `<<` operator.

The following example uses the member function `write()`:

```
const int MAX_CHARS = 80;
char cName[MAX_CHARS + 1] = "Namir Shammas";
int nNumChars = strlen(cName) + 1;
fstream f;
f.open("MYDATA.DAT:, ios::out | ios::binary);
// write the number of characters
f.write((const unsigned char*)&nNumChars,
    sizeof(nNumChars));
// write the characters
f.write((const unsigned char*)cName, nNumChars);
f.close();
```

This example opens the file MYDATA.DAT for binary output by sending the C++ message `open()` to the object f (an instance of class `fstream`). The last two executable statements write the number of output characters, and then the characters themselves, by sending the C++ message `write()` to the object f. The arguments for the first `write()` message are the typecasted address of the variable nNumChars and the expression `sizeof(nNumChars)`. The arguments for the second `write()` message are the string variable cName and the variable nNumChars.

Read member function

The class `istream` declares the member function `read()` as follows:

```
istream& read(char* pch, int nCount);
istream& read(unsigned char* puch, int nCount);
istream& read(signed char* psch, int nCount);
```

The parameters pch, puch, and psch are pointers to a character array. The parameter nCount specifies the maximum number of characters to read. The member function extracts bytes from the stream until the limit nCount is reached or until the end of file is reached. The member function `read()` is useful for binary stream input. For text input, use the member function `getline()`.

The following example uses the member function `read()`:

```
const int MAX_CHARS = 80;
char cName[MAX_CHARS + 1] = "Namir Shammas";
int nNumChars = strlen(cName) + 1;
fstream f;
```

```
f.open("MYDATA.DAT:, ios::out | ios::binary);
// read the number of characters
f.read((const unsigned char*)&nNumChars,
    sizeof(nNumChars));
// read the characters
f.read((const unsigned char*)cName, nNumChars);
f.close();
```

This example opens the file MYDATA.DAT for binary input by
sending the C++ message open() to the object f (an instance of
class fstream). The last two executable statements read the
number of input characters, and then the characters themselves,
by sending the C++ message read() to the object f. The arguments
for the first read() message are the typecasted address of the
variable nNumChars and the expression sizeof(nNumChars).
The arguments for the second read() message are the string
variable cName and the variable nNumChars.

Sequential Text Stream I/O

The C++ stream library offers the operators << and >> and the
member function getline() to support text stream I/O. The
declaration of member function getline() is as follows:

```
istream& getline(char* pszStr, int nCount, char
    cDelim = '\n');
istream& getline(signed char* pszStr, int nCount,
    char cDelim = '\n');
istream& getline(unsigned char* pszStr, int nCount,
    char cDelim = '\n');
```

The parameter pszStr is a pointer to an ASCIIZ string, which is a
string that contains readable text and ends with the null character.
The parameter nCount specifies the maximum number of input
characters. The parameter cDelim specifies the string delimiter.

The following example uses the member function getline() as
part of the file I/O:

```
const int MAX_CHARS = 81;
char aLine[MAX_CHARS];
fstream f;
f.open("README.DOC", ios::in);
while (!f.eof()) {
 f.getline(aLine, MAX_CHARS);
 cout << aLine << endl;
}
f.close();
```

This example opens the file AUTOEXEC.BAT for text input. The code contains a `while` loop that reads each line in the file and displays it on the console. The input operation uses the member function `getline()`.

Stream Library

The C++ stream library contains the class `ios`. This class declares identifiers that set the file stream mode. The following table shows the file modes that are exported by the class `ios`.

The C++ stream library has the classes `ifstream`, `ofstream`, and `fstream` to support input file stream, output file stream, and both input and output file stream. You typically use the class `fstream` to create file stream objects.

Identifier	Meaning
`ios::app`	Open stream to append data
`ios::ate`	Set stream pointer to the end of the file
`ios::binary`	Open in binary mode
`ios::in`	Open stream for input
`ios::nocreate`	Generate an error if the file does not already exist
`ios::noreplace`	Generate an error if the file already exists
`ios::out`	Open stream for output
`ios::trunc`	Truncate the file size to 0 if it already exists

Part V

Decision-Making

This part looks at making decisions in C++ programs with the if and switch statements. These statements empower your applications to examine the values of variables and determine whether to carry out a task or which specific task to perform. C++ supports a versatile if statement that supports single, dual, and multiple alternatives.

In this part . . .

- ✔ Using the if statement
- ✔ Working with the if-else statement
- ✔ Using the multiple-alternative if statement
- ✔ Working with the switch statement

If Statement

C++ offers the if statement, which allows you to make a decision based on the logical value of an expression. The simplest version of the if statement is the *single-alternative* version. This form of the if statement performs a task when a tested condition is true. When the tested condition is false, the task is not performed. The general syntax for the if statement is as follows:

```
if (condition)
 statements
```

The preceding syntax shows that the single-alternative if statement contains the following parts:

- ✦ The keyword if.

- ✦ A set of parentheses that contains the tested condition. This condition is a logical expression that evaluates to 0 (false) or nonzero (true).

- ✦ The *statements,* which can be one or more statements. Programmers call multiple statements a *statement block,* or a set of statements enclosed in a pair of braces — { }. The program executes these statements when the tested condition is true.

The following examples show how the single-alternative if statement works:

```
if (j < 0)
 j = 0;
k = 2 * j;

if (k >= 0 && k <= 9) {
 j = 2 * k;
 m = k * k;
}
k += 3;
```

The first if statement tests whether the variable j stores a negative value. If this condition is true, the program first executes the statement that assigns 0 to the variable j and then executes the statement that assigns 2 * j to the variable k. By contrast, if the tested condition is false (that is, the variable j stores a non-negative number), the program execution skips the statement that assigns 0 to variable j and proceeds to the assignment statement that stores a new value in variable k.

The second if statement tests whether the variable k stores an integer in the range of 0 to 9. If this condition is true, the program executes the statement block — which contains the two assignment statements — and then resumes with the statement that increments the value in the variable k. By contrast, if the integer stored in the variable k falls outside the range of 0 to 9, the program execution skips the statement block and resumes at the last assignment statement (k += 3;).

The program IF1.CPP prompts you for your age and uses an if statement to determine whether you can vote in an upcoming election (in which only people 18 and older can vote). The following is the source code for the program IF1.CPP:

```
/* IF1.CPP

A C++ program that illustrates
a single-alternative if statement
*/

#include <iostream.h>

main()
{
  int Age;

  // prompt you to enter your age
  cout << "Enter your age : ";
  cin >> Age;

  // display leading part of message
  cout << "You can";
  // is your age less than 18?
  if (Age < 18)
  cout << "not"; // display not clause
  // display tail part of message
  cout << " vote\n";

  return 0;
}
```

This simple example shows the single-alternative if statement at work. The following is a sample session with the program (I underlined user input):

```
Enter your age : 16
You cannot vote
```

In IF1.CPP, the function main() declares the int-type variable Age. The function performs the following tasks:

✦ Prompts you for your age.

✦ Accepts your input and stores it in the variable Age.

✦ Displays the message You can as the leading part of the output message.

✦ Uses a single-alternative if statement to determine whether the variable Age stores a value that is less than 18 (the minimum voting age). If the tested condition is true, the program executes the statement in the if clause, which displays the word not as the middle part of the output message. By contrast, if the variable Age stores an integer that is 18 or higher, the program skips the output statement in the if clause. In other words, if Age is at least 18, the output does not include the word not.

✦ Displays the word vote as the last part of the message.

If-Else Statement

C++ also supports a version of the if statement that allows you to take alternative actions. The *dual-alternative* if *statement* examines a condition and then chooses between two alternatives. If the tested condition is true, the program executes one (or more) statements. If the condition is false, the program executes another set of statements. The general syntax for the dual-alternative if (or if-else) statement is as follows:

```
if (condition)
  first statement or statement block
else
  second statement or statement block
```

The preceding syntax shows that the dual-alternative if statement contains the following parts:

✦ The keyword if.

✦ A set of parentheses containing the tested condition. This condition is a logical expression that evaluates to 0 (false) or nonzero (true).

✦ The first statement or statement block, which the program executes when the tested condition is true.

✦ The keyword else, which marks the start of the statement (or statement block) for the alternative action.

✦ The second statement or statement block, which the program executes when the tested condition is false. I refer to this statement (or statement block) as the else clause.

The following example shows how the dual-alternative if statement works:

```
if (myChar >= 'a' && myChar <= 'z')
  cout << "Character is a lowercase letter\n";
else
  cout << "Character is not a lowercase letter\n";
```

The preceding example examines the contents of the variable myChar to determine whether it stores a lowercase letter. When this condition is true, the program executes the output statement in the if clause (this statement displays the message Character is a lowercase letter). By contrast, when the variable myChar does not store a lowercase letter, the program executes the output statement in the else clause, which displays the message Character is not a lowercase letter.

The next set of statements shows the source code for the IF2.CPP program. The program prompts you for your age and uses an if statement to determine whether you can vote in an upcoming election (in which only those who are 18 or older can vote). The following is the source code for the program IF2.CPP:

```
/* IF2.CPP

 A C++ program that illustrates
 a dual-alternative if statement
*/

#include <iostream.h>

main()
{
  int Age;

  // prompt you to enter your age
  cout << "Enter your age : ";
  cin >> Age;

  // is your age less than 18?
  if (Age < 18)
  cout << "You cannot vote\n";
  else
  cout << "You can vote\n";

  return 0;
}
```

This example shows the dual-alternative if statement at work. The following is a sample session with the program (the under-lined value is your input to this session):

```
Enter your age : 19
You can vote
```

In this code, the function `main()` declares the `int`-type variable Age. The function performs the following tasks:

✦ Prompts you for your age.

✦ Accepts your input and stores it in the variable Age.

✦ Uses a dual-alternative `if` statement to determine whether the variable Age stores a value that is less than 18 (the minimum voting age). If the tested condition is true, the program executes the statement in the `if` clause, which displays the words You cannot vote. By contrast, if the variable Age stores an integer that is 18 or higher, the program executes the output statement in the `else` clause, which displays the words You can vote.

Multiple-Alternative If Statement

C++ supports a special nested form of the `if` statement — one that's even more versatile than the forms described in the preceding sections. The *multiple-alternative* `if` *statement* allows you to test a series of conditions and execute the statement blocks associated with the first condition that is true. The general syntax for the multiple-alternative `if` statement is as follows:

```
if (condition1) {
 statement set #1
}
else if (condition2) {
 statement set #2
}
else if (condition3) {
 statement set #4
}
...
else {
catch-all statement set
}
```

The preceding syntax shows that the multiple-alternative `if` statement contains the following parts:

✦ The keyword `if`.

✦ A set of parentheses that contains the first tested condition. This condition is a logical expression that evaluates to 0 (false) or nonzero (true).

✦ The first statement set (statement set #1), which the program executes when the tested condition1 is true. The program execution then resumes after the `if` statement — that is, after the last `else` clause.

♦ The first set of `else if` keywords, which precede the second tested condition (condition2). This statement is the second `if` statement, which appears in the `else` clause of the first `if` statement.

♦ A set of parentheses that contains the second tested condition. This condition is a logical expression that evaluates to 0 (false) or nonzero (true).

♦ The statement set #2, which the program executes when the tested condition2 is true. The program execution then resumes after the `if` statement.

♦ Other `else if` clauses that contain their own tested conditions and statement sets to execute. Each new `if` statement appears in the `else` clause of the `if` statement that precedes it.

♦ The keyword `else`, which indicates the start of the catch-all clause. This clause covers anything other than the conditions that the program tests. Although this clause is optional, I highly recommend that you use one in your multiple-alternative `if` statements.

♦ The catch-all statement set, which the program executes when all of the tested conditions (in the `if` clause and the `else if` clauses) are false.

The following example shows how the multiple-alternative `if` statement works:

```
unsigned Num;
cout << "Enter a non-negative integer : ";
cin >> Num;
if (Num >= 0 && Num <= 9)
 cout << "Input is a single digit\n";
else if (Num >= 10 && Num <= 99)
 cout << "Input is a double digit\n";
else if (Num >= 100 && Num <= 999)
 cout << "Input is a triple digit\n";
else
 cout << "Input is 1000 or greater\n";
```

This example declares an `unsigned`-type variable `Num` and uses it to store a number that you enter. The example then uses a multiple-alternative `if` statement to determine whether the value of the integer stored by the variable `Num` has one, two, three, or more digits.

The preceding source code performs the following actions:

+ The if statement first tests whether the variable Num contains an integer in the range from 0 to 9. If this condition is true, the program executes the output statement in the if clause, which displays the message Input is a single digit.

+ If the first tested condition fails, the program moves to the first else if clause. This clause tests whether the variable Num contains an integer in the range from 10 to 99. If this condition is true, the program executes the output statement in the first else if clause, which displays the message Input is a double digit.

+ If the second tested condition fails, the program execution proceeds to the second else if clause. This clause tests whether the variable Num contains an integer in the range from 100 to 999. If this condition is true, the program executes the output statement in the second else if clause, which displays the message Input is a triple digit.

+ If the third tested condition fails, the program execution proceeds to the catch-all else clause. This clause executes the output statement that displays the message Input is 1000 or greater.

The following example shows a nested if statement supporting multiple alternatives. The statements show the source code for the IF3.CPP program. The program prompts you for your age and uses an if statement to determine what kind of character (that is, either lowercase, uppercase, or digit) you enter.

The following is the source code for the program IF3.CPP:

```
/* IF3.CPP

 A C++ program that illustrates
 a multiple-alternative if statement
*/

#include <iostream.h>

main()
{
 char inputChar;

 cout << "Enter a character : ";
 cin >> inputChar;
```

```
// examine input character using
// multiple-alternative if statement
if (inputChar >= 'a' && inputChar <= 'z')
cout << "You entered a lowercase character\n";
else if (inputChar >= 'A' && inputChar <= 'Z')
cout << "You entered an uppercase character\n";
else if (inputChar >= '0' && inputChar <= '9')
cout << "You entered a digit\n";
else
cout << "You entered a non-alphanumeric
  character\n";

return 0;
}
```

The following is a sample session with the program (the under-lined value is your input):

```
Enter a character : 5
You entered a digit
```

The statements contain the function main( ), which declares the char-type variable inputChar. The function performs the following tasks:

+ Prompts you to enter a character.

+ Stores your input in the variable inputChar.

+ Uses a multiple-alternative if statement to examine the character in the variable inputChar. The if statement starts by testing whether the variable inputChar contains a lowercase character (that is, a character in the range of *a* to *z*). If this condition is true, the program displays the message You entered a lowercase character.

+ Uses the first else if clause, when the first condition fails, to test whether the variable inputChar contains an upper-case character (that is, a character in the range of *A* to *Z*). If this condition is true, the program displays the message You entered an uppercase character.

+ Uses the second else if clause, when the second condition fails, to test whether the variable inputChar contains a digit (that is, a character in the range of 0 to 9). If this condition is true, the program displays the message You entered a digit.

+ Uses the catch-all else clause, when all the preceding conditions fail, to execute the output statement that displays the message You entered a non-alphanumeric character.

Multiple-Alternative Switch Statement

For a simpler approach than that of the multiple-alternative if statement, C++ offers the *multiple-alternative* switch *statement*. The switch statement compares a variable's value with integers, characters, or enumerated values and then executes a set of statements based on the outcome of the comparison. The general syntax for the switch statement is as follows:

```
switch (variableName) {
  case value1_1:
  [case value1_2:
  case value1_3:
  ...
  case value1_N1:]
  statement set #1
  [break;]

  case value2_1:
  [case value2_2:
  case value2_3:
  ...
  case value2_N2:]
  statement set #2
  [break;]

  [other case label sets]

  default:
  statement set # N
}
```

The preceding syntax shows that the switch statement contains the following parts:

+ The keyword switch.

+ The variable to examine (called the *switch variable*), which is enclosed in a set of parentheses.

+ The body of the switch statement, which is enclosed in a pair of braces ({}). The body of the switch statement contains one or more sets of case labels and a statement block following each set. Each case label begins with the keyword case, followed by a constant and a colon. The program compares the value of the switch variable with each value in a set of case labels. If the switch variable matches any value in a set, the program executes the statement block that is associated with that set.

+ A break statement, which follows each statement block. Although the break statement is technically optional, you rarely find a switch statement without break statements.

The break statement causes the program flow to resume after the switch statement. Otherwise, the program flow resumes at the *next* statement block.

✦ The catch-all default: clause, which the program executes when the value of the switch variable fails to match any value in the various sets of case labels.

The switch statement compares the value of the switch variable with the values in every set of case labels. If the switch variable matches any case value in a set, the program executes the statements that are associated with that set of case labels. Each set of statements typically ends with the break statement, which prevents the program from executing the remaining statements in the switch statement. Using the break statement allows the switch statement to behave more like a multiple-alternative if statement.

The following is an example of a switch statement:

```
switch (Num) {
  case 0:
  case 2:
  case 4:
  case 6:
  case 8:
  cout << "Digit is even\n";
  break;

  case 1:
  case 3:
  case 5:
  case 7:
  case 9:
  cout << "Digit is odd\n";
  break;

  default:
  cout << "Not a single digit\n";
}
```

The preceding switch statement uses the variable Num as the switch variable. The switch statement has two sets of case labels and the default clause. The first set of case labels compares the value of the variable Num with 0, 2, 4, 6, and 8. If the value in that variable matches any of these values, the program executes the output statement that displays the message Digit is even and then executes the break statement. This statement resumes program execution after the end of the switch statement. In other words, if the program finds a match in this first set of case labels, it skips the second set of case labels and the default: clause and resumes execution with any statements that follow this switch statement.

The second set of case labels in the switch statement compares the value in the variable Num with 1, 3, 5, 7, and 9. If the value in that variable matches any of these values, the program executes the output statement that displays the message Digit is odd and then executes the break statement. This statement resumes program execution after the switch statement. The default clause executes the output statement that displays the message Not a single digit.

The preceding switch statement is equivalent to the following if statement:

```
if (Num == 0 || Num == 2 || Num == 4 ||
 Num == 6 || Num == 8)
  cout << "Digit is even\n";
else if (Num == 1 || Num == 3 || Num == 5 ||
 Num == 7 || Num == 9)
  cout << "Digit is odd\n";
else
  cout << "Not a single digit\n";
```

Note that reading the switch statement is much easier than reading the if statement.

TIP

Use the if statement to compare a variable (or expression) with a wide range of values.

The next set of statements show the source code for the SWITCH.CPP program. The program prompts you to select a menu item by number and uses a switch statement to determine which menu command you want to invoke. The following is the source code for the program SWITCH.CPP:

```
/* SWITCH.CPP

  A C++ program that illustrates
  a switch statement
*/

#include <iostream.h>

main()
{
  int Choice;

  // prompt user with simulated menu
  cout << " Simulated Menu\n";
  cout << "———————————\n\n";
  cout << "1. Quit\n\n";
  cout << "2. Open a new file\n\n";
  cout << "3. Open an existing file\n\n";
  cout << "Select choice by number : ";
  // get the menu number
  cin >> Choice;
  cout << "\n\n";
```

```
// examine choice
switch (Choice) {
case 1:
cout << "Exiting program\n";
break;

case 2:
cout << "Opening a new file . . .\n";
break;

case 3:
cout << "Opening an existing file . . .\n";
break;

default:
cout << "Sorry! Bad menu selection\n";
}

return 0;
}
```

This example shows the switch statement at work. The following is a sample session with the program (the underlined value is your input):

```
Simulated Menu
_____

1. Quit

2. Open a new file

3. Open an existing file

Select choice by number : 2

Opening a new file . . .
```

This code shows the function main(), which declares the int-type variable Choice. The function performs the following tasks:

- ✦ Displays the simple menu by using a set of output statements.

- ✦ Prompts you to select a menu choice by number.

- ✦ Stores your numeric menu choice in the variable Choice.

- ✦ Uses a switch statement to examine the value in variable Choice. The switch statement has three sets of case labels (each set has a single value) and the default clause.

    The first case label compares the value in the variable Choice with 1. The statement associated with that case label displays the message Exiting program. The second case label compares the value in the variable Choice with 2. The statement associated with that case label displays the message Opening a new file . . . The third case label compares the value in the variable Choice with 3. The statement associated with that case label displays the message Opening an existing file . . . The default: clause contains the output statement that displays the message Sorry! Bad menu selection.

Part VI

Loops

Loops allow you to repeat tasks multiple times. These tasks can be simple or complex. This part looks at loops that iterate for a preset number of times and loops that iterate as long as a tested condition is true. This part also includes information about how to exit loops and how to nest them.

In this part . . .

- ✔ Using the do-while loop
- ✔ Exiting loops
- ✔ Working with the for loop
- ✔ Nesting loops
- ✔ Skipping loop iterations
- ✔ Using the while loop

Do-While Loop

The do-while loop is a conditional loop. This kind of loop tests the loop continuation condition *after* it executes the loop's statements. The loop continues to iterate as long as the loop's condition remains true. Because the loop's condition is at the end of the loop, the do-while loop executes its statements at least once. The general syntax for the do-while loop is as follows:

```
do {
  statements
} while (condition);
```

The following is an example of a do-while loop:

```
int j = 1;
double sum = 0;
do {
  sum += j;
  j++;
} while (j < 1001);
```

The preceding code declares the int-type variable j and initializes it with the value 1. The code also declares the variable sum and initializes it with the value 0. The loop has two statements. The first statement adds the value of variable j to variable sum. The second statement increments the value in variable j by 1. After executing the loop statements, the do-while loop checks whether the value in variable j is less than 1,001. As the loop iterates, the value in variable j increases from 1 (the initial value) to 1,000. Thus, the do-while loop adds the integers from 1 to 1,000.

Because the do-while loop tests a condition after it executes the loop's statements, the loop always executes its statements at least once. The following example shows a do-while loop that executes its statements once:

```
int j = 2000;
double sum = 0;
do {
  sum += j;
  j++;
} while (j < 1001);
cout << "After the loop\n";
```

The preceding code declares the int-type variable j and initializes it with the value 2,000. The code also declares the variable sum and initializes it with the value 0. The do-while loop executes two statements and then tests the condition j < 1001. Because the variable j (which has the initial value of 2,000) becomes 2,001 after executing the second statement in the loop, the condition of the loop fails. Consequently, the program execution resumes at the output statement.

When the condition of the do-while loop is erroneously written to be always true, the loop iterates endlessly. The same effect occurs when the variables used to test the loop's condition never change values in the loop's statements.

To show you how do-while loops work, the following is a program that prompts you to enter a range of positive integers to add. This program uses do-while loops to ensure that you enter the proper integer values to define the range of positive integers that you want the program to add. This program shows a somewhat practical side of using the do-while loops (that is, making sure that an input value lies in a specific range of values).

The following is the source code for the DOWHILE.CPP program:

```
/* DOWHILE.CPP

A C++ program that illustrates
a simple do-while loop
*/

#include <iostream.h>

main()
{
  int Num1, Num2;
  double Sum = 0;

  do {
  cout << "Enter the lower (and positive) limit : ";
  cin >> Num1;
  } while (Num1 <= 0);

  do {
  cout << "Enter the higher (and positive)
    limit : ";
  cin >> Num2;
  } while (Num1 > Num2);

  for (int i = Num1; i <= Num2; i++)
  Sum += i;

  cout << "The sum of integers from "
<< Num1 << " to " << Num2
  << " = " << Sum << "\n";

  return 0;
}
```

The following is a sample session that uses the DOWHILE.CPP program (the underlined characters indicate your input to this session):

```
Enter the lower (and positive) limit : 1
Enter the higher (and positive) limit : 1000
The sum of integers from 1 to 1000 = 500500
```

The preceding statements show the function main( ), which declares the int-type variables Num1 and Num2 as well as the double-type variable Sum. The function performs the following tasks:

+ Uses a do-while loop to prompt you for a positive integer that defines the lower limit for the range of numbers that you want to add. The loop contains two statements. The first statement displays the prompt message, while the second statement accepts your input and stores it in the variable Num1. The loop tests whether the value in variable Num1 is negative or zero. Thus, the loop iterates only once if you enter a positive integer the first time. Otherwise, the loop iterates as long as you continue to input anything other than a positive integer.

+ Uses a do-while loop to prompt you for a positive integer that defines the upper limit for the range of numbers that you want to add. The loop contains two statements. The first statement displays the prompt message, while the second statement accepts your input and stores it in the variable Num2. The loop tests whether the value in variable Num1 exceeds that in variable Num2. Thus, the loop iterates only once if you enter a proper positive integer the first time. Otherwise, the loop iterates as long as your input falls below the value that you entered for the lower range limit.

+ Adds the integers in the range of values defined by the variables Num1 and Num2. This task uses a for loop and the loop control variable i. The loop alters the values of the loop control variable between the values in variables Num1 and Num2. The loop adds the value of the control variable to the value in the variable Sum.

+ Displays the range of integers to add (in variables Num1 and Num2) and their sum (in variable Sum).

Exiting Loops

C++ allows you to exit the current loop using the break statement. This statement causes the program to resume immediately after the end of the current loop (which can be a `for`, `while`, or `do-while` loop). The following is an example of using the `break` statement to exit from a loop:

```
int nVal;
do {
 cout << "Enter a positive integer ";
 cin >> nVal;
 if (nVal > 0)
 break;
 cout << "You must enter a positive integer" <<
    "\n";
} while (nVal < 1);
```

This example uses a `do-while` loop to prompt you to enter a positive integer. The loop stores your input in the variable `nVal`. The loop uses an `if` statement to determine whether the variable contains a positive integer. When this condition is true, the loop executes the `break` statement, which exits the loop. Otherwise, the loop displays a reminder to enter a positive integer and then reiterates.

Use the `break` statement sparingly — it makes the loop's code hard to follow.

The following program, EXITLOOP.CPP, uses the `break` statement to exit from a loop. This program has a `for` loop that is set to iterate between 0 to 100. However, the program exits the loop when the loop control variable reaches the value of 9.

```
/* EXITLOOP.CPP

 A C++ program that illustrates
 exiting a loop using the break statement
*/

#include <iostream.h>

main()
{
 const int MIN_VAL = 0;
 const int MAX_VAL = 100;
 const int CRITICAL_VAL = 9;

 for (int i = MIN_VAL; i <= MAX_VAL; i++) {
 cout << "i = " << i << "\n";
 if (i == CRITICAL_VAL)
 break;
 }

 return 0;
}
```

The following is the output from the EXITLOOP.CPP program:

```
i = 0
i = 1
i = 2
i = 3
i = 4
i = 5
i = 6
i = 7
i = 8
i = 9
```

The function main() declares the int-type constants MIN_VAL, MAX_VAL, and CRITICAL_VAL. The first two constants define the range of iteration, whereas the last one defines the critical value that is used to exit the loop. The function contains a for loop that uses the variable i as a control variable. The loop is supposed to iterate between the values defined by constants MIN_VAL and MAX_VAL. However, the loop contains an if statement that compares the loop control variable with the value of the constant CRITICAL_VAL. When the two values match, the if statement executes the break statement, causing the program to exit the loop after iterating only ten times.

For Loop

To repeat tasks a fixed number of times, you use the for loop. The general syntax for the for loop is as follows:

```
for (loop initialization part; loop continuation
    test; loop update part)
  statements
```

The preceding syntax shows that the loop starts with the keyword for, followed by parentheses that enclose the following parts and their roles:

✦ The *loop initialization part* sets the initial values for the variables (the for loop allows you to use several variables) that control the number of iterations. Programmers call these variables *loop control variables.* The program executes this part only once. (Be aware that the comma operator is used to initialize multiple loop control variables.) You can declare a loop control variable in this part, and the variable remains accessible until the end of the current loop's scope.

✦ The *loop continuation test* checks the values of the loop control variables to determine whether to perform another iteration. By performing this loop continuation test before each iteration, the program decides whether it should repeat the loop.

✦ The *loop update part* updates the value of the loop control variable after each loop iteration.

Interestingly, the three parts of the `for` loop are optional. As a beginning C++ programmer, you should write all three parts of the loop and thus make your loops more readable. As you get more comfortable with C++, you can omit some of these parts and use other statements in their place.

A `for` loop with no initialization, loop continuation, or loop update parts is called an *open loop, infinite loop,* or *endless loop.* This loop iterates endlessly. To prevent endless iteration, use an `if` statement that invokes a `break` statement to exit when the conditions are right (depending on what the loop does).

The following examples illustrate the roles of the three parts of the `for` loop. The following loop performs its statements 1,000 times to add the numbers from 1 to 1000:

```
double sum = 0;
for(int i = 1; // initialize variable to 1
   i <= 1000; // test whether variable is less than
   // or equal to 1000
   i++) // increment loop control variable by 1
   sum += i;
```

The loop initialization part declares the loop control variable `i` and sets its initial value to 1; the program performs this task just once. The loop continuation test determines whether the variable `i` is less than or equal to 1,000. The program performs this task before it executes the assignment statement (`sum += i;`). Next, the loop update part increases the value in the variable `i` by 1. The program performs this task after it ends a loop iteration. Therefore, the loop increases the value in the variable `i` from 1 to 1,000 in increments of 1. The result is that the loop iterates 1,000 times. The loop adds the integers in the range of 1 to 1,000.

Consider the following `for` loop:

```
double sum = 0;
for(int i = 1; // initialize variable to 1
   i <= 1000; // test whether variable is less than
   // or equal to 1000
   i += 2) // increment loop control variable by 2
   sum += i;
```

The preceding loop initializes its control variable with the value 1, continues to iterate while the control variable is less than or equal to 1,000, and increments the loop control variable by 2. Thus, the loop iterates 500 times and, in effect, adds the odd integers in the range of 1 to 1,000.

The preceding `for` loops increase the values of their control variables. This kind of loop is called an *upward-counting fixed loop*. The following is an example of a downward-counting loop, which essentially performs the task of adding odd integers:

```
double sum = 0;
for(int i = 999; // initialize variable to 999
  i > 0; // test whether variable is greater than 0
  i -= 2) // decrement loop control variable by 2
  sum += i;
```

The preceding loop initializes the loop control variable to the value 999, the upper limit. Next, the loop continuation test determines whether the loop control variable contains a value greater than 0 (because 1 is the last integer to be added to the variable `sum`). The loop update part decreases the value of the control variable by 2.

You can declare the loop control variables before the `for` loop starts, as shown in the following example:

```
double sum = 0;
int i;
for(i = 1; // initialize variable to 1
  i <= 1000; // test whether variable is less than
  // or equal to 1000
  i++) // increment loop control variable by 1
  sum += i;
```

The following program, FOR1.CPP, works with a simple, upward-counting for loop.

```
/* FOR1.CPP

  A C++ program that illustrates
  a simple for loop
*/

#include <iostream.h>

main()
{
  const int MAX_LINES = 9;

  for (int i = 1; i <= MAX_LINES; i++)
    cout << "Line number " << i << "\n";

  return 0;
}
```

This program uses a `for` loop to display the following nine lines:

```
Line number 1
Line number 2
Line number 3
Line number 4
Line number 5
Line number 6
Line number 7
Line number 8
Line number 9
```

The source code in FOR1.CPP declares the constant MAX_LINES inside the function main( ). The function contains a `for` loop that declares the control variable i. The loop initializes this variable to 1. Next, the loop continuation test determines whether the loop control variable has a value less than or equal to the value of the constant MAX_LINES. The loop update part increases the value of the loop control variable by 1. Therefore, the loop iterates with values in the variable i ranging from 1 to MAX_LINES. The loop has a single statement that displays an output line.

Nesting Loops

C++ allows you to nest loops in any combination. For example, you can nest `for` loops, as shown in the following code:

```
double fSum = 0;
for (int i = 10; i < 100; i++)
  for (int j = 1; j < i; j++)
  fSum += double(j * i);
```

These statements show two nested `for` loops that are used to obtain the sum of the product of two arbitrary ranges of numbers.

You can also nest different kinds of loops. The following code shows nested `while` and `do-while` loops:

```
double fSum = 0;
int i = 10;
int j;
while (i < 100) {
  j = 0;
  do {
  fSum += double(j++ * i);
  } while (j < i);
  i++;
  }
```

The nested loops obtain a summation as did the loop in the example of the nested `for` loops.

The following program, NESTED.CPP, uses nested loops. This program prompts you to enter two positive integers that define a range of numbers to add. The program displays the sums of integers from 1 to the numbers that you entered.

The following is the source code for the NESTED.CPP program:

```
/* NESTED.CPP

   A C++ program that illustrates
   nested for loops
*/

#include <iostream.h>

main()
{
  int Num1, Num2;
  double Sum;

  do {
  cout << "Enter the lower (and positive) limit : ";
  cin >> Num1;
  } while (Num1 <= 0);

  do {
  cout << "Enter the higher (and positive)
      limit : ";
  cin >> Num2;
  } while (Num1 > Num2);

  // obtain sum
  for (int i = Num1; i <= Num2; i++) {
  Sum = 0; // initialize summation
  for (int j = 1; j <= i; j++)
  Sum += j;
  cout << "The sum of integers from 1 to "
       << i << " = " << Sum << "\n";
  }

  return 0;
}
```

The following is a sample session of the program (with user input underlined):

```
Enter the lower (and positive) limit : 10
Enter the higher (and positive) limit : 15
The sum of integers from 1 to 10 = 55
The sum of integers from 1 to 11 = 66
The sum of integers from 1 to 12 = 78
The sum of integers from 1 to 13 = 91
The sum of integers from 1 to 14 = 105
The sum of integers from 1 to 15 = 120
```

The function `main()` declares the `int`-type variables `Num1` and `Num2`, which store the lower and higher limits for the summations. The function also declares the `double`-type variable `Sum` to store the summations (one at a time). Note that the highlight of the program is the nested `for` loops, which calculate and display the summations. The outer `for` loop uses the variable `i` as the control variable and iterates between the values in variables `Num1` and `Num2`. First, the loop assigns 0 to the variable `Sum` to prepare it for summing numbers. The inner `for` loop uses the variable `j` and iterates between the values of 1 and `i`. Next, the inner loop has one statement that adds the value of variable `j` to the variable `Sum`. The last statement in the outer loop displays the range of added integers and the value of the sum of these integers (stored in the variable `Sum`).

Skipping Loop Iterations

C++ offers the `continue` statement to skip the remaining statements in the current loop. Why skip the remaining statements in a loop? This condition arises when the loop statements examine a condition and conclude that the loop should not or need not proceed with executing the remaining statements. The following is an example of using the `continue` statement:

```
for (int i = -4; i < 5; i++) {
 if (i == 0)
continue;
 double fX = 1.0 / i;
 cout << "1 / " << i << " = " << fX << "\n";
}
```

This code shows a loop that displays reciprocal values. The loop has a control variable that changes values from −4 to 4, in increments of 1. This loop contains an `if` statement that determines whether the control variable contains 0. When this condition is true, the loop skips the remaining statements to avoid dividing by zero.

While Loop

C++ offers the `while` loop, which is a conditional loop. This type of loop tests the loop continuation condition *before* it executes the loop's statements. The loop continues to iterate as long as the loop's condition remains true. The general syntax for the `while` loop is as follows:

```
while (condition)
 statements
```

The following example shows how a while loop works:

```
int j = 1;
double sum = 0;
while (j < 1001) {
  sum += j;
  j++;
}
```

The preceding code declares the int-type variable j and initializes it with the value 1. The code also declares the variable sum and initializes it with the value 0. If the value in the variable j is less than 1,001, the while loop executes its loop statements.

The loop contains two statements. The first statement adds the value of variable j to the variable sum, while the second one increments the value in variable j by 1. As the loop iterates, the value in variable j increases from 1 (the initial value) to 1,000. Therefore, the while loop adds the integers between 1 and 1,000.

A while loop may skip its loop statements entirely. Remember that a while loop tests a condition *before* it executes the loop statements. If the tested condition is false from the outset, the loop statements are never executed.

Make sure that the loop alters the value(s) of the variables that are in the tested condition. Otherwise, the loop iterates endlessly, because nothing affects the values in the tested condition.

The following example shows a while loop that does not execute its statements:

```
int j = 2000;
double sum = 0;
while (j < 1001) {
  sum += j;
  j++;
}
cout << "After the loop\n";
```

The preceding code declares the int-type variable j and initializes it with the value 2,000. The code also declares the double-type variable sum and initializes that variable with the value 0. The while loop tests whether the value in variable j is less than 1,001. Because the variable j has an initial value of 2,000, the condition of the loop fails. Consequently, the program execution skips the loop statements and resumes at the output statement.

The following source code shows you the WHILE.CPP program. This program uses the `while` loop to determine whether you entered a vowel. If you enter a nonvowel character, the loop reminds you to enter a vowel.

```
/* WHILE.CPP

 A C++ program that illustrates
 using a while loop
*/

#include <iostream.h>

// declare prototype
int isNotVowel(char);

main()
{
 char Letter;

 cout << "Enter a vowel : ";
 cin >> Letter;

 while (isNotVowel(Letter)) {
 cout << "\nPlease enter a vowel : ";
 cin >> Letter;
 }

 cout << "\nYou entered " << Letter << "\n";

 return 0;
}

int isNotVowel(char c)
{
 return (c != 'a' &&
 c != 'e' &&
 c != 'i' &&
 c != 'o' &&
 c != 'u' &&
 c != 'A' &&
 c != 'E' &&
 c != 'I' &&
 c != 'O' &&
 c != 'U');
}
```

The following is a sample session with this program (the underlined characters identify your input to this session):

```
Enter a vowel : d
Please enter a vowel : f
Please enter a vowel : a
You entered a
```

These statements declare the functions isNotVowel() and main(). The function isNotVowel() determines whether its argument is a nonvowel. The function has an int return type and the single char-type parameter c. The function determines whether the argument for parameter c is not a vowel and returns true if this is the case. Otherwise, the function yields false. The function has a single return statement with a Boolean expression.

The function main() declares the char-type variable Letter and performs the following tasks:

◆ Prompts you to enter a vowel.

◆ Accepts your input and stores it in the variable Letter.

◆ Uses a while loop to determine whether your input is a nonvowel. The condition of the loop is the result that is returned by calling the function isNotVowel(). The loop supplies the variable Letter as the argument for the function isNotVowel(). Note that the while loop contains two statements. The first statement is an output statement that reprompts you to enter a vowel. The second statement is an input statement that accepts your input and stores it in the variable Letter. This loop iterates as long as the function isNotVowel() returns a nonzero value (that is, as long as you enter a nonvowel character).

◆ Displays the vowel that you entered.

Part VII

Data Types, Enumerated Types, and Data Structures

Data types empower your applications to organize the bits of zeros and ones into more useful information, such as numbers, characters, strings, and so on. This part shows you how to use predefined data types and how to create your own data types.

The predefined data types represent the most basic data types that come with C++. These data types support logical values, characters, integers, and floating-point numbers.

You can create various kinds of data types that fit your own needs. These custom data types build on predefined data types and other previously defined custom data types. You can also create a kind of data type that relates a list of constants to describe enumerated values or states of some objects.

In this part . . .

- ✔ Using predefined data types
- ✔ Working with enumerated types
- ✔ Using structures
- ✔ Working with unions

Data Types (Predefined)

C++ supports a collection of predefined data types. The following subsections cover these predefined data types.

Boolean data type

C++ supports the `bool` type, which represents a Boolean type. This data type is relatively new to C++ compilers. Older compiler versions use 0 to represent false and any nonzero value to represent true. The new generation of C++ compilers support the `bool` type, which has the `true` and `false` values. The compiler regards the values `true` and `false` as 1 and 0, respectively.

Here is an example of using the type `bool`:

```
main()
{
   bool bIsOdd;
   int nNum;

   cout << "Enter a positive integer : ";
   cin >> nNum;
   bIsOdd = (nNum % 2) > 0;
if (bIsOdd)

     cout << "You entered an odd number\n";
   else
     cout << "You entered an even number\n";

   return 0;
}
```

This example has function `main()` declare the `bool`-type variable `bIsOdd` and the `int`-type variable `nNum`. The function prompts you to enter a positive integer and stores that input in variable `nNum`. The function then assigns the Boolean result of the expression `(nNum % 2) > 0` to the variable `bIsOdd`. The function then uses an `if-else` statement to display text that indicates whether your input was an odd or an even number. The `if` statement uses the variable `bIsOdd` to select the appropriate text for display.

Character data type

C++ offers the character data type by using the identifier `char`. This data type supports a single character, such as the letters *A, b,* and *X* and the punctuation symbols ! and #. You use characters, for example, to display a currency symbol (such as $), a percent sign (the % character), or a pound sign (the # character) as part of the output to the screen. C++ requires you to enclose character literals in a pair of single quotation marks. The following are examples of characters:

```
'A'
'x'
'?'
'\n'
```

The first example is the character literal for the letter *A*. The second example is a character literal for the letter *x*. Next, the third example is a character literal for the question mark (?). Finally, the fourth example shows a special character, the new line character.

C++ supports special *escape sequence characters* that begin with the backslash character (\) and are followed by one or more characters. The characters \n represent the new line character. The following table shows the escape sequence characters.

Sequence	Task
\a	Beep
\b	Backspace
\f	Form feed
\n	New line
\r	Carriage return
\t	Horizontal tab
\v	Vertical tab
\\	Backslash
\'	Single quote
\"	Double quote
\?	Question mark

I now present a program that uses and displays character literals. The following source code is for the CHARTYPE.CPP program.

```
/* CHARTYPE.CPP

   A C++ program that shows how to use the character
   type literals
*/

#include <iostream.h>

main()
{
```

(continued)

(continued)

```
// lowercase character
cout << 'a' << "\n";

// uppercase character
cout << 'X' << "\n";

// digit
cout << '5' << "\n";

// special new line character
cout << '\n';

// punctuation character
cout << '!' << "\n";

    return 0;
}
```

The preceding program generates the following output:

```
a
X
5

!
```

   ✦ The first output statement displays the character *a* by sending
     the character literal 'a' to the output screen.

   ✦ The second output statement displays the character *X* by
     sending the character literal 'X' to the output screen.

   ✦ The third output statement displays the digit 5 by sending the
     character literal '5' to the output screen.

   ✦ The fourth output statement displays a blank line by sending
     the special character '\n' to the output screen.

   ✦ The last output statement displays the exclamation mark by
     sending the character literal '!' to the output screen.

Floating-point data types

C++ supports *floating-point data types,* which are float, double,
and long double. Floating-point data types support numbers
with decimals. You can use these data types, for example, to
perform scientific, statistical, engineering, and financial
calculations.

The following table describes the floating-point data types.

Data Type	Comment	Range (For Turbo C++ Lite)	Examples
float	Single-precision floating-point	$3.37 \times 10^{+38}$ to 8.43×10^{-37}, 0, and -8.43×10^{-37} to $-3.37 \times 10^{+38}$	5.25, −478.25, −1.3e+30, 3.4e−12, 34.5F
double	Double-precision floating-point	15.258, − $2.225074 \times 10^{-308}$, 0, $-2.225074 \times 10^{-308}$ to $-1.797693 \times 10^{+308}$	$1.797693 \times 10^{+308}$ to 5.2e+300, −789.2154
long double	Extended-precision floating-point	$1.1 \times 10^{+4932}$ to 3.4×10^{-4932}, 0, -3.4×10^{-4932} to $-1.1 \times 10^{+4932}$	7.58e+3123

The most common floating-point data type used by C++ programmers is double. This type supports the double-precision floating-point and is therefore preferred over the single-precision float type. Compared to single-precision, double-precision stores numbers more accurately (because it stores more digits) and covers a wider range of numbers.

Notice that, in the previous table, the last example in the type float (the number 34.5F) contains a floating-point number with the *F* suffix. This suffix tells the compiler to treat the number as a single-precision number.

The following program displays floating-point literals. The source code for the REALTYPE.CPP program is as follows.

```
/* REALTYPE.CPP

    A C++ program that shows how to use the
    floating-point
    type literals
*/

#include <iostream.h>

main()
{
  // single-precision floating-point number
  cout << 12.34F << "\n";

  // double-precision floating-point number
  cout << 12.34 << "\n";

  // single-precision floating-point number
  // in scientific format (using e exponent)
  cout << 1.234e+30 << "\n";

  // single-precision floating-point number
  // in scientific format (using E exponent)
  cout << 1.234E+30 << "\n";
```

(continued)

(continued)

```
// double-precision floating-point number
// in scientific format (using e exponent)
cout << 1.234e+300 << "\n";

// double-precision floating-point number
// in scientific format (using E exponent)
cout << 1.234E+300 << "\n";

return 0;
}
```

This program generates a set of integers. Here's what the output looks like:

```
12.34
12.34
1.234e+30
1.234e+30
1.234e+300
1.234e+300
```

+ The first output statement sends the single-precision floating-point number 12.34F. Notice that, even though the output is 12.34, the constant itself includes the letter F, which tells the compiler to use single precision with this number.

+ The second output statement sends the double-precision floating-point number 12.34. The second statement appends the letter L after the number 12.34 to tell the compiler that the number is a double-precision floating-point number. The letter L affects the way that the compiler stores the number but not how it appears on the screen. In other words, you don't see additional trailing zeros, even though the number is a double-precision floating-point number.

+ The third output statement displays the single-precision floating-point number 1.234e+30, which is in scientific format (that is, 1.234×10^{30}). The statement uses the lowercase e exponent character.

+ The fourth output statement is similar to the third one. The main difference is that the fourth statement uses the upper-case E exponent character. Both statements generate the output 1.234e+30. You can work with either a lowercase or an uppercase E; the compiler reads them as being the same character.

+ The fifth output statement displays the double-precision floating-point number 1.234e+300 in scientific format. This statement uses the lowercase e exponent character.

✦ The final output statement is similar to the fifth one. The main difference is that the final statement uses the uppercase E exponent character. Both statements generate the output 1.234e+300.

Integer data types

C++ supports different kinds of *integer data types* (that is, whole numbers) that differ from each other by the range of values that they encompass. The following table shows the various kinds of integers. This table includes a column that shows the various integer types as well as the range of values for each type based on a 16-bit system (such as DOS and Windows 3.1). In the case of 32-bit systems (such as Windows 95 and Windows NT), the int type doubles the range of values compared to the range in 16-bit systems. In other words, an int on a 16-bit system has the same range of values as a short int, while the 32-bit int has the same range of values as a long int on a 16-bit system. The C++ compiler enables you to omit the keyword int when used with short, long, unsigned, and signed. Thus, for example, long has the same meaning as long int. Likewise, unsigned means the same thing as unsigned int.

C++ Keywords for Data Type	Comment	Value Range	Examples
int	Integer	−32768 to 32767	1234, −5463, 0
short int	Short integer	−32768 to 32767	−122, 123, 0
short unsigned int, unsigned short int	Unsigned short	0 to 65535	210, 129, 22
long int	Long integer	−2147483648 to 2147483647	65536, 1000000, −54632, 4L
unsigned int	Unsigned integer	0 to 65535	65000, 8U, 16u
long unsigned int, unsigned long int	Unsigned long integer	0 to 4294967295	123456, 4567788, 70000

Why does C++ support multiple integer data types? Why not have just one integer data type? The answer is that each integer data type uses a specific amount of memory to store a numeric value. The narrower that the range of values of an integer data type is, the less memory it requires and vice versa. Therefore, if you work with integers that range from 0 to 100, it makes more sense to use the `short int` type (which uses less memory to store the value) rather than the `long int` type (which uses more memory).

The previous table shows that C++ uses the identifier `int` to define the basic integer type. This table also reveals that C++ uses the following *type modifier keywords* (that is, identifiers reserved by the C++ language) to alter the range of integers:

◆ `short` declares a short integer that has the smallest range of values compared to the other integer data types.

◆ `long` declares a long integer that has the largest range of values compared to the other integer data types.

◆ `unsigned` declares that the integer type has no negative values.

◆ `signed` declares that the integer type has both positive and negative values. By default, integer types are signed; therefore, you rarely need to use the signed-type modifier.

The most common integer type abbreviations used by programmers are `long` and `unsigned`, which refer to signed long integers and unsigned integers.

A few notes about declaring long and unsigned integer literals: The table that appears earlier in this section on "Integer data types" shows a few interesting examples, particularly the literals `4L`, `8U`, and `16u`, which show the suffixes L, U, and u. Appending the suffix L to an integer literal tells the C++ compiler to treat that literal (usually a small value, such as 4 or 873) as a long integer and not a standard integer (compatible with the data type `int`). Likewise, appending the suffix U (or u) to an integer literal tells the C++ compiler to treat that literal as an unsigned integer and not as a standard integer.

If the suffix L isn't used with small-value integers, the compiler treats that value as a standard integer. You use the suffix L because you want to promote the data type that is used for the literal integer to make it compatible with other integers in the same statement. For example, `70000 + 34L` adds two long integer numbers, one of which is promoted to a long integer.

Never use the letter `l` (el) as a suffix for a literal, because that letter is easily mistaken for the number 1 (one).

A *literal* is an explicit (or verbatim) value. Literal values are to programming language what gold is to currency. For example, the number `10` is a *literal integer*. Another example is the letter `X`, which is a *literal character.* The following is the source code for the INTTYPE.CPP program, which uses and displays integers:

```
/* INTTYPE.CPP

   A C++ program that shows how to use the integer
   type literals
*/

#include <iostream.h>

main()
{
  // short signed integer
  cout << 12 << "\n";

  // signed integer
  cout << -12000 << "\n";

  // signed long integer
  cout << 655350L << "\n";

  // unsigned integer
  cout << 65535u << "\n";

  return 0;
}
```

This program generates the following output:

```
12
-12000
655350
65535
```

The program contains a source code that defines the function main(). Every C++ program needs the function main(), because that function begins program execution. The function contains four output statements:

✦ The cout << 12 << "\n"; statement sends the short signed integer 12 to the screen. The object cout represents the screen. The << command sends a value to the screen.

✦ The cout << -12000 << "\n"; statement sends the signed integer -12000 to the screen.

✦ The cout << 655350L << "\n"; statement sends the long integer 655350 to the screen.

Notice that the third output statement appends the letter L after the digits 655350 to tell the compiler that this integer literal is a long integer.

◆ The `cout << 65535u << "\n";` statement displays the unsigned integer 65535.

Notice that the last output statement appends the letter u after the digits 65535 to tell the compiler that this integer literal is an unsigned integer.

The previous program shows you how to use and display integer literals. As you discover more about programming C++, you find out how to integrate displaying integer literals with other kinds of information.

String data type

A *string* is a chain of text that stores messages or names of data items. While the core C++ language does not define a string type (as do most other languages, such as Basic and Pascal), C++ supports string literals. A string literal is a chain of characters enclosed in quotation marks. The following are examples of string literals:

```
" "
"Hi there! How are you?"
"Hello world!\nHow are you?\n"
"\n\n"
```

The first example shows an empty string literal. The second statement shows a rather typical string literal. The third example shows a string literal that contains the special \n new line (or *carriage return*) characters. Finally, the last example is a string that contains two carriage return characters.

Notice that C++ distinguishes between literal characters (such as `'A'` and `'@'`) and single-character strings (such as `"A"` and `"@"`). Therefore, the constant `'A'` is a character, for example, whereas the constant `"A"` is a string.

The following program, STRTYPE.CPP, uses and displays string literals:

```
/* STRTYPE.CPP

   A C++ program that shows how to use the string
   type literals
*/

#include <iostream.h>

main()
{
  // string message followed by "\n"
  cout << "Hello world!" << "\n";
```

```
    // string message includes \n character
    cout << "Hello world!\n";

    // fragmented string message on the one line
    cout << "Hello"  " world" "!" "\n";
    // fragmented string message on multiple lines
    cout << "Hello"
            " world" "!"
            "\n";
    return 0;
}
```

This program generates the following output:

```
Hello world!
Hello world!
Hello world!
Hello world!
```

Using three slightly different statements, you've told the program to generate the same message four times.

+ The first output statement displays the `Hello world!` message by sending the string literal `"Hello world!"` to the output screen. The statement also emits the new line characters `\n` in a separate string that is located in the same statement.

+ The second output statement displays the `Hello world!` message by sending the string literal `"Hello world!\n"` to the output screen (that is, the standard output stream object `cout`). Notice that the string literal also contains the new line characters `\n`.

+ The third output statement displays the `Hello World!` message by sending the string literals `"Hello"`, `" world"`, `"!"`, and `"\n"` to the output screen (that is, the standard output stream object `cout`). Notice that the statement contains a set of string literals on the same line. The C++ compiler treats the chained set of string literals as if it were one string literal.

+ The last output statement displays the `Hello World!` message by sending the string literals `"Hello"`, `" world"`, `"!"`, and `"\n"` to the output screen (that is, the standard output stream object `cout`). Notice that the statement contains a set of string literals on multiple lines. The C++ compiler treats this kind of chained set of string literals as though it were one string literal. Obviously, it makes no difference to the C++ compiler whether the chained string literals are on the same line or spread over multiple lines.

The previous program shows you that C++ is flexible enough to support displaying strings in many ways. The last two output statements show you that you can display a string as a set of string literals that appear either on the same line or on different lines. Therefore, the program shows you that you can break a lone piece of text into smaller string literals and place each literal on a separate line.

Void data type

C++ has a special data type called void. This data type represents a none-of-the-above data type. In other words, the type void is not an integer type, a floating-point type, a character type, or a user-defined type (that is, a data type that you define). For now, you need to know only that C++ supports the predefined void type. You find out more about this type in upcoming parts that deal with functions.

Type definition in C++

You often use data types in a programming language, especially the basic predefined ones, in different contexts. For example, the int type serves as an array index, a counter for a number of items, pixel coordinates, and even a logical value. C++, like its parent language C, enables you to create alias types that makes your source code easier to read and comprehend. The typedef statement creates the data type aliases and has the following syntax:

```
typedef oldType newType;
```

The oldType parameter represents a previously defined type (either a predefined data type or a user-defined data type). The newType parameter represents the new alias. The following are examples of the typedef statement:

```
// Example 1
typedef int Color;
// Example 2
typedef int ArrayIndexType;
// Example 3
typedef int NumberOfElemsType;
// Example 4
typedef double WeightType;
// Example 5
typedef double SalaryType;
// Example 6
typedef double AreaType;
```

Example 1 uses the `typedef` statement to create the `Color` type
as an alias type for `int`. Using the `Color` type identifier is clearer
than using `int` for variables and parameters that store color-
related data. For example, the prototype of function `show1` is a bit
easier to read than function `show2`:

```
void show1(ColorUseColor);
void show2(int UseColor);
```

Example 2 uses the `typedef` statement to create the type
`ArrayIndexType` as an alias for `int`. Again, using the
`ArrayIndexType` is clearer than using `int` for variables and
parameters that represent array indices.

Example 3 uses the `typedef` statement to create the type
`NumberOfElemsType` as an alias for `int`. Once more, using the
`NumberOfElemsType` is clearer than using `int` for variables and
parameters that represent number of elements in an array.

Similarly, examples 5, 6, and 7 use the `typedef` statement to
create the types `WeightType`, `SalaryType`, and `AreaType` as
aliases to the predefined type `double`. Using these alias types
brings a clearer meaning to their related variables and parameters.

C++ enables you to create aliases for single-dimensional and
multidimensional arrays. The general syntax for this kind of alias
type is as follows:

```
typedef basicElemType
    sdArrayType[numberOfElements];
typedef basicElemType
    mdArrayType[Elems1][Elems2]...;
```

The `typedef` statement creates a single-array type by stating the
type of the basic element of the array, the array name, and the
number of elements. In the case of a multidimensional array, the
`typedef` statement lists the size of each dimension.

The following are examples of creating array type aliases:

```
// example 1
typedef int weekDays[7];
// example 2
const int MAX_ROWS = 25;
const int MAX_COLS = 80;
typedef char textScreen[MAX_ROWS][MAX_COLS];
```

Example 1 defines the alias array type `weekDays` as an `int`-type
array of 7 elements. The second example defines the alias matrix
type `textScreen` as a `char`-type matrix of `MAX_ROWS` and
`MAX_COLS`.

To define variables and parameters by using the alias array type merely requires using the name of the alias array type. You must not include the number of array elements. The following are examples of using the alias types weekDays and textScreen:

```
main()
{
  weekDays theDays; // array of 7 in-type elements
  textScreen theScreen // matrix of characters
  // other statements
}
```

Enumerated Types

You can declare a single constant by using the const keyword. C++ allows you to create a list of logically related constants that enumerate a set of values or states. The following is the general syntax for declaring an enumerated type:

```
enum enumeratedType { enumerator1, enumerator2, ...
    };
```

The declaration of an enumerated type starts with the keyword enum and is followed by the name of the enumerated type identifier and the list of *enumerators*. This comma-delimited list is enclosed in braces and ends with a semicolon.

What about the values that are associated with the enumerators? By default, the compiler assigns 0 to the first enumerator, 1 to the second one, and so on. The following section describes how you can assign explicit values to some or all of the enumerators.

The following are examples of declaring enumerated types:

```
// example 1
enum weekDays { Sunday, Monday, Tuesday, Wednesday,
  Thursday, Friday, Saturday };
// example 2
enum colors { red, blue, green, yellow, brown };
// example 3
enum CPUtype { Intel_8086, Intel_80286,
  Intel_80386, Intel_80486, Intel_Pentium };
```

The first example declares the weekDays type with the names of the weekdays as the enumerators. The compiler assigns the value 0 to the enumerator Sunday, 1 to the enumerator Monday, and so on.

The second example declares the enumerated type colors and specifies the enumerators red, blue, green, yellow, and brown. The compiler assigns 0 to the enumerator red, 1 to the enumerator blue, and so on. The last example declares the enumerated type `CPUtype` and lists the names of a number of Intel chips. The compiler assigns 0 to the enumerator `Intel_8086`, 1 to the enumerator `Intel_80286`, and so on.

C++ enables you to assign integer values to enumerators. Make sure that the given constants resolve to integers between –32,768 and +32,767 (signed) or between 0 and +65,535 (unsigned). Otherwise, the compiler generates a warning.

C++ requires you to observe the following features and rules when assigning explicit values to enumerators:

✦ The values must be within the ranges that were previously indicated.

✦ The values that are assigned to the enumerators need not be unique. Only the enumerator's identifiers must be unique.

✦ The values that are assigned need not follow an ascending or descending numeric pattern. You can assign numbers in an arbitrary manner.

✦ The compiler assigns values to the enumerators that have no explicit value. In this case, the value that is assigned to an enumerator equals 1 plus the value of the previous enumerator (or 0, if the enumerator is the first one).

The following are examples of enumerated types with explicit values:

```
enum weekDay { Sunday = 1, Monday, Tuesday,
    Wednesday,
  Thursday, Friday, Saturday };
enum digits { Five = 5, Four = 4, Three = 3, Zero =
    0,
  One, Two, Six = 6, Seven, Eight, Nine };
```

The first example shows the enumerated type `weekDay` and assigns the value 1 to the enumerator `Sunday`. Next, the compiler assigns the value 2 to the enumerator `Monday`, 3 to the enumerator `Tuesday`, and so on.

The second example shows a more elaborate use of the explicit values feature. The enumerated type `digits` explicitly assigns the integers 5, 4, 3, and 0 to the enumerators `Five`, `Four`, `Three`, and `Zero`, respectively. Then the compiler assigns 1 and 2 to the enumerators `One` and `Two`, respectively. The declaration then assigns 6 to the enumerator `Six`. Finally, the compiler assigns 7, 8, and 9 the enumerators `Seven`, `Eight`, and `Nine`, respectively.

When you declare and use variables and parameters that have enumerated types, you must explicitly assign new values to these variables and parameters. Avoid using the arithmetic operators or increment operators with enumerated types, because the enumerators in these types may not be associated with sequential values (such as 1, 2, 3, 4, and so on).

Here is an example using an enumerated type to declare variables:

```
enum weekDay { Sunday = 1, Monday, Tuesday,
    Wednesday,
  Thursday, Friday, Saturday };
weekDay myDay = Monday;

if (myDay != Sunday && myDay != Saturday)
  myDay = Saturday;
```

This example declares the variable myDay as having the enumerated type weekDay. The declaration of that variable also initializes it by using the enumerator Monday. The if statement determines if the variable myDay is neither enumerator Sunday nor Monday. When this condition is true, the if statement assigns the enumerator Saturday to the variable myDay.

Remember that, within the same program, enumerators are unique names. To resolve name conflicts, use enumerated types that are nested in classes or in namespaces. You can then use the name of the class or the namespace to qualify the enumerators. For example, you can have two weekDay types declared in two classes (for example, Class1 and Class2). Then you can refer to Sunday as either Class1::Sunday or Class2::Sunday without raising a compiler error.

Structures

C++ supports user-defined structures. The following sections discuss the syntax for declaring and using structures.

Declaring structures

The general syntax for declaring a structure type is as follows:

```
struct structureName
{
 type1 dataMember1;
 type2 dataMember2;
 other data members
};
```

The structure declares its data members, which have either predefined data types or previously defined types (such as enumerated types, other structures, unions, arrays, and so on).

The following are examples of structures:

```
struct Point
{
 double m_fX;
 double m_fY;
};

struct Rectangle
{
 Point m_UpperLeftCorner;
 Point m_LowerRightCorner;
 double m_fLength;
 double m_fWidth;
};

struct Person
{
 char m_cFirstName[10];
 char m_cMiddleInitial;
 char m_cLastName[15];
 int m_BirthYear;
 double m_fWeight;
};
```

The structure Point has the two double-type data members
m_fX and m_fY. The structure Rectangle has the Point-type
data members m_UpperLeftCorner and m_LowerRightCorner
and the double-type data members m_fLength and m_fWidth.
The structure Rectangle is an example of a structure that
contains data members that are themselves structures. The
structure Person has the following data members:

+ The member m_cFirstName, which is an array of 10 characters that stores the first name

+ The char-type member m_cMiddleInitial, which stores
  the middle initial character

+ The member m_cLastName, which is an array of 10 characters that stores the last name

+ The int-type member m_BirthYear, which stores the birth
  year

+ The double-type member m_fWeight, which stores the
  weight

The structure Person is an example of a structure that contains
data members that are arrays.

Declaring structured variables

Declaring structured variables is no different than declaring variables with predefined types. The following is the general syntax of structured variables:

```
// declaring a single variable
structuredType structuredVariable;
// declaring an array of structures
structuredType structuredArray[numberOfElements];
```

The following are examples of declaring structured variables, using the structures that I declared in the previous section:

```
Point Origin, StartPoint, EndPoint, Points[10];
Rectangle myRectangle;
Person Me, You, Us[30];
```

These examples declare the Point-type variables Origin, StartPoint, and EndPoint. The example also declares the Point-type array Points to have 10 elements. Furthermore, the example declares the Rectangle-type variable myRectangle, the Person-type variables Me and You, and the Person-type array Us.

Accessing structure members

Accessing the data members of a structure uses the dot operator (which looks like a period). The general syntax for accessing the data member of a structure is as follows:

```
structuredVariable.dataMember
```

When you access the members of a structure with a pointer, use the -> operator. The general syntax for accessing the data member of a structure by using a pointer is as follows:

```
pointerToStructured->dataMember
```

The following are examples of accessing the data members of structures:

```
struct Point
{
  double m_fX;
  double m_fY;
};

struct Rectangle
{
  Point m_UpperLeftCorner;
  Point m_LowerRightCorner;
  double m_fLength;
  double m_fWidth;
};
```

```
Rectangle Shape;
Rectangle* pShape = &Shape;

// set the coordinates for the upper left corner
Shape.m_UpperLeftCorner.m_fX = 10.5;
Shape.m_UpperLeftCorner.m_fY = 12.5;
// set the coordinates for the lower right corner
Shape.m_LowerRightCorner.m_fX = 50.5;
Shape.m_LowerRightCorner.m_fY = 5.5;
pShape->m_fLength = Shape.m_UpperLeftCorner.m_fX -
  Shape.m_LowerRightCorner.m_fX;
pShape->m_fWidth = Shape.m_LowerRightCorner.m_fY -
  Shape.m_UpperLeftCorner.m_fY;
```

This code declares the structured variable Shape and a pointer to that variable pShape. The example accesses the data members m_fLength and m_fWidth by using the pointer pShape in the expressions pShape->m_fLength and pShape->m_fWidth, respectively. To access the nested data members m_fX and m_fY, the code uses two dot operators, one to access the data member m_UpperLeftCorner or m_UpperRightCorner and the other to access the nested data members m_fX or m_fY.

Initializing structures

C++ enables you to initialize the data members of a structures. This feature resembles initializing arrays and follows similar rules. The general syntax for initializing a structured variable is as follows:

```
structuredType structuredVariable = { value1,
  value2, . . .};
```

The compiler assigns value1 to the first data member of the variable structuredVariable, value2 to the second data member of the variable structuredVariable, and so on. You need to observe the following rules:

✦ The assigned values should be compatible with their corresponding data members.

✦ You can declare fewer initialing values than data members. The compiler assigns zeros to the remaining data members of the structured variable.

✦ You cannot declare more initializing values than data members.

✦ The initializing list sequentially assigns values to data members of nested structures.

✦ The initializing list assigns values sequentially to data members that are arrays.

Keep in mind that initializing structures is as simple or as complex as the initialized structures themselves.

The following are examples of initializing structures:

```
struct Point
{
 double m_fX;
 double m_fY;
};

struct Rectangle
{
 Point m_UpperLeftCorner;
 Point m_LowerRightCorner;
 double m_fLength;
 double m_fWidth;
};

Point FocalPoint = { 12.4, 34.5 };
Rectangle Shape = { 100.0, 50.0, 200.0, 25.0 };

// calculate the length
Shape.m_fLength = Shape.m_UpperLeftCorner.m_fX -
 Shape.m_LowerRightCorner.m_fX;
// calculate the width
Shape.m_fWidth = Shape.m_LowerRightCorner.m_fY -
 Shape.m_UpperLeftCorner.m_fY;
```

These statements declare the structures `Point` and `Rectangle`. The example also declares the `Point`-type variable `FocalPoint` and initializes its data members `m_fX` and `m_fY` with the values `12.4` and `34.5`. The example also declares the `Rectangle`-type `Shape` and initializes the first two data members `m_UpperLeftCorner` and `m_LowerRightCorner`. Each of these data members requires two initializing values, because they have the type `Point`. Therefore, the compiler assigns the values `100.0`, `50.0`, `200.0`, and `25.0` to `Shape.m_UpperLeftCorner.m_fX`, `Shape.m_UpperLeftCorner.m_fX`, `Shape.m_LowerRightCorner.m_fX`, and `Shape.m_LowerLeftCorner.m_fX`, respectively.

Copying structured variables

C++ permits the assignment operator to copy the values of one structured variable into another variable that has the same type. Therefore, you can copy into a single statement multiple data members that include arrays and nested structures.

The following is an example of how to copy structured variables:

```
struct Point
{
 double m_fX;
 double m_fY;
};

main()
{
 Point Coord1, Coord2;
 // assign values to first structure variable
 Coord1.m_fX = 1;
 Coord1.m_fY = 2;
 // copy structures
 Coord2 = Coord1;

 return 0;
}
```

This code shows that the function main() declares the structured variables Coord1 and Coord2. The function assigns values 1 and 2 to the data members m_fX and m_fY, respectively, in the variable Coord1. The function then copies the values in that variable to Coord2. Thus the data members m_fX and m_fY in variable Coord2 also store the values 1 and 2, respectively.

The assignment operator performs a *shallow copy* when applied to structured variables. A shallow copy involves copying, bit by bit, the values in the data members of the source variable to the corresponding data members in the target variable. The potential problem with this kind of copying arises when you have data members that are pointers (that is, variables that hold addresses) to other data. In this case, you have more than one structured variable with members that point to the same piece of information. What happens if you update the address of the pointer in one variable but not the other? You end up with corrupted addresses!

Unions

Unions are special kinds of structures that overlay the space of their data members. The size of a union equals the size of its largest data member. C++ offers unions that are compatible with the C language. However, unions were more popular in the days of limited memory resources.

C++ has inherited unions from its parent language C. Unions were popular a few decades ago, because they save memory space by storing one or multiple data types in the same space. In today's age of megabytes of memory, unions have lost much of their appeal.

98 *Unions*

Unions serve two main purposes. The first is to conserve memory space by storing different kinds of mutually exclusive information. The second purpose is to perform data conversion by using data members that access parts of other data members in the same union. The general syntax for declaring a union type is as follows:

```
union unionName
{
  type1 dataMember1;
  type2 dataMember2;
  other data members
};
```

The union declares its data members, which have either pre-defined data types or previously defined types (such as enumerated types, structures, other unions, arrays, and so on). The following are examples of unions:

```
union XInt
{
  long m_lInt;
  int m_nInt[2];
};

union XFloat
{
  float m_fX;
  double m_lfX;
}
```

The first example declares the union XInt, which has the long-type data member m_lInt and the two-element array int-type data member m_nInt. Because the size of a long is equal to twice the size of an int, the size of the union XInt is equal to sizeof(long) [which is also equal to 2 * sizeof(int)].

The second example declares the union XFloat with its float-type and double-type data members m_fX and m_lfX, respectively. Because the double type occupies more space than the float type, the size of the union XFloat is equal to the size of the double type.

Declaring union variables and accessing data members in unions is very similar to doing the same thing in structures.

Remember: The data members in unions do not occupy neighboring memory locations as in structures. Instead, they store their data in the same location. That's why you can use only one data member at a time in a union.

As with structures, C++ considers unions as special kinds of classes. You can include constructors in unions and use member functions to extract information from a union variable.

Part VIII

Arrays

Arrays are special variables that store multiple values. You can access each value by using one or more indices. Arrays are perhaps the simplest and yet most powerful data structures that many programming languages support. C++ supports single-dimensional and multidimensional arrays as well as operators for dynamic arrays. The following sections provide a reference for dynamic, multidimensional, and single-dimensional arrays.

In this part . . .

✔ **Working with dynamic arrays**

✔ **Using multidimensional arrays**

✔ **Working with single-dimensional arrays**

Dynamic Arrays

Dynamic arrays are arrays that you can create and remove at runtime. C++ offers the operators new and delete (see Part I) to create and remove dynamic arrays, respectively. The general syntax for creating a dynamic array is as follows:

```
pointerToArray = new dataType[NumberOfElements];
```

This syntax shows that you need to use a pointer to manage a dynamic array. The operator new creates the dynamic array. The operator requires that you specify the data type of the array elements and the number of elements. The operator new returns the address of the dynamic array or yields null if the allocation fails. This kind of failure occurs with insufficient memory.

You must allocate the space for a dynamic array before attempting to use the pointer that is associated with it. Remember that if the allocation fails, that pointer is null.

The following is an example of creating a dynamic array:

```
const int MAX = 10;
int pArr = new int[MAX];
```

This code declares the int-type constant MAX and then uses that constant to create a dynamic array in the second statement. Next, the second statement declares an int-type pointer pArr and initializes that pointer with the address of the dynamic array. The statement uses the operator new to create an int-type dynamic array that has MAX elements.

To remove a dynamic array, C++ offers the operator delete. The general syntax for using the operator delete is as follows:

```
delete [] pointerToArray;
```

This syntax shows that the operator delete needs to have a pair of empty brackets followed by the name of the pointer that is accessing the dynamic array. The empty brackets tell the compiler that the operator is deleting a dynamic array.

You must remove a dynamic array after you are done working with it to reclaim the memory space that it uses.

The following is an example of removing a dynamic array:

```
delete [] pArr;
```

This code removes a dynamic array that is accessed by the pointer pArr.

Accessing the elements of a dynamic array uses the pointer to the array and an index. C++ supports the following two forms:

```
pointerToArray[index]
*(pointerToArray + index)
```

The first form uses a syntax that resembles that of nondynamic arrays. Then the second syntax uses a C-style form. This syntax shows that the C++ compiler treats the name of a static array or a pointer to a dynamic array as the address of the first element of the static array and dynamic array, respectively.

The following program, DARRAY1.CPP, creates, uses, and then removes a dynamic array. The program performs the following tasks:

+ Prompts you to enter the number of elements (used to create a dynamic array of integers)

+ Prompts you to enter integers for the dynamic array

+ Displays the array elements in the order that you entered them

+ Sorts the array elements

+ Displays the elements of the sorted array

+ Removes the dynamic array

The DARRAY1.CPP source code is as follows:

```
/* DARRAY1.CPP

   A C++ program that illustrates
   creating and accessing a dynamic array
   using a pointer
*/

#include <iostream.h>

main()
{
  const int MIN_ELEMS = 4;
  const int MAX_ELEMS = 10;
  int nNumElems;
  int *arrayPtr;
  int i, j, k, nSwapBuffer;

  // prompt user for the number of elements
  do {
    cout << "Enter the number of elements ["
         << MIN_ELEMS << " to " << MAX_ELEMS
         << "] : ";
    cin >> nNumElems;
```

(continued)

(continued)

```
  } while (nNumElems < MIN_ELEMS || nNumElems >
  MAX_ELEMS);

  // create the dynamic array
  arrayPtr = new int[nNumElems];

  // prompt the user to enter nNumElems integers
  for (i = 0; i < nNumElems; i++) {
    cout << "Enter integer # " << i << " : ";
    cin >> arrayPtr[i];
  }

  cout << "Initial array is : ";
  for (k = 0 ; k < nNumElems; k++)
    cout << arrayPtr[k] << " ";
  cout << "\n";

  // sort the array
  for (i = 0; i < (nNumElems - 1); i++) {
    for (j = i+1; j < nNumElems; j++) {
      if (arrayPtr[i] > arrayPtr[j]) {
        nSwapBuffer = arrayPtr[i];
        arrayPtr[i] = arrayPtr[j];
        arrayPtr[j] = nSwapBuffer;
      }
    }
  }

  cout << "Sorted array is : ";
  for (k = 0 ; k < nNumElems; k++)
    cout << *(arrayPtr + k) << " ";
  cout << "\n";

  // delete dynamic array
  delete [] arrayPtr;

  return 0;
}
```

The following is a sample session with the program:

```
Enter the number of elements [4 to 10] : 5
Enter integer # 0 : 67
Enter integer # 1 : 65
Enter integer # 2 : 41
Enter integer # 3 : 48
Enter integer # 4 : 25
Initial array is : 67 65 41 48 25
Sorted array is : 25 41 48 65 67
```

The function main() declares a set of constants and variables that are used to manage the dynamic array. In particular, the int-type pointer arrayPtr accesses the elements of the dynamic array. The function main() performs the following tasks:

- ✦ Prompts you to enter the number of elements in the range that is defined by the values of constants MIN_ELEMS and MAX_ELEMS. This task uses a do-while loop to ensure that your input (which the function stores in variable nNumElems) is in the specified range. The loop iterates (repeats) as long as your input is outside that range.

- ✦ Creates the dynamic array by using the operator new. This task creates an int-type array with nNumElems elements. The function assigns the address of the dynamic array to the pointer arrayPtr.

- ✦ Prompts you to enter the values for each element in the dynamic array. This task uses a for loop that has the loop control variable i. The loop stores each number that you enter in an element of the dynamic array. The input statement stores your input in element number i using the expression arrayPtr[i].

- ✦ Displays the values in the dynamic array by using a for loop. This task accesses each array element by using the expression arrayPtr[k], where k is the loop control variable.

- ✦ Sorts the array by using nested for loops. These loops compare and swap (if necessary) the elements of the dynamic array.

- ✦ Displays the values that are in the sorted dynamic array by using a for loop. This task accesses each array element by using the expression arrayPtr[k], where k is the loop control variable.

- ✦ Removes the dynamic array by using the operator delete. This task applies the operator delete to the pointer arrayPtr.

Multidimensional Arrays

C++ enables you to declare arrays that have multiple dimensions. You access the elements of these arrays by using multiple indices – one index for each dimension. The most popular kind of multidimensional arrays are the ones with two dimensions. You can think of this kind of array as a table of rows and columns. Another type of multidimensional array is one with three dimensions. You can think of this kind of array as a three-dimensional cube of data or an array of tables.

Accessing multidimensional arrays

After you declare a multidimensional array, you can access its elements by using the index operator [ ]. The general syntax for accessing an element in an array is as follows:

```
arrayName[IndexOfDimension1][IndexOfDimension2]...
```

The indices for the various dimensions should be in the valid ranges — between 0 and the number of array elements for the dimension minus one.

The following is an example of accessing multidimensional array elements:

```
const int MAX_ROWS = 10;
const int MAX_COLS = 20;
double fMatrix[MAX_ROWS][MAX_COLS];
for (int i = 0; i < MAX_ROWS; i++)
  for (int j = 0; j < MAX_COLS; j++)
    fMatrix[i][j] = double(2 + i 2 * j)
```

This code declares the constants MAX_ROWS and MAX_COLS and uses these constants in declaring the double-type two-dimensional array fMatrix. Therefore, the array has rows with indices in the range of 0 to MAX_ROWS - 1 and columns with indices in the range of 0 to MAX_COLS - 1. The code uses nested for loops to initialize the elements of the array fMatrix. Notice that the last assignment statement uses the expression fMatrix[i][j].

Declaring multidimensional arrays

C++ requires you to declare a multidimensional array before you use it. The general syntax for declaring a multidimensional array is as follows:

```
type
    arrayName[numberOfElement1][numberOfElement2]_;
```

This syntax shows the following aspects:

◆ The declaration starts by stating the basic type that is associated with the array elements. You can use predefined (by C++) or previously defined (by the user) data types.

◆ The name of the array is followed by a sequence of the number of elements for the various dimensions. These numbers appear in brackets. Each number of elements must be a constant (literal or symbolic) or an expression that uses constants.

All multidimensional arrays in C++ have indices that start at 0. Therefore, the number of array elements in each dimension is one value higher than the index of the last element in that dimension.

The following are examples of declaring multidimensional arrays:

```
// example 1
int nIntCube[20][10][5];
// example 2
```

```
const int MAX_ROWS = 50;
const int MAX_COLS = 20;
double fMatrix[MAX_ROWS][MAX_ROWS];
// example 3
const int MAX_ROWS = 30;
const int MAX_COLS = 10;
char cNameArray[MAX_ROWS+1][MAX_COLS];
```

The first example declares the int-type three-dimensional array nIntCube with 20 by 10 by 5 elements. This declaration uses the literal constants 20, 10, and 5. Therefore, the indices for the first dimension are in the range of 0 to 19. The indices for the second dimension are in the range of 0 to 9. Finally, the indices for the third dimension are in the range of 0 to 5.

The second example declares the constants MAX_ROWS and MAX_COLS and uses these constants to specify the number of rows and columns of the double-type matrix fMatrix.

The third example declares the char-type matrix cNameArray. The constant expression MAX_ROWS + 1 defines the number of rows in the array cNameArray. Then the constant MAX_COLS defines the number of columns in the array cNameArray.

Initializing multidimensional arrays

C++ enables you to initialize some or all of the elements in a multidimensional array. The general syntax for initializing a multidimensional array is as follows:

```
type arrayName[numberOfElement1][numberOfElement2]
    = { value0 ,..., valueN };
```

Be aware of the following in initializing a multidimensional array:

✦ The list of initial values appears in a pair of braces and is comma-delimited.

✦ The list may contain a number of initial values that are equal to or less than the total number of elements that are in the initialized array. Otherwise, the compiler generates a compile-time error.

✦ The compiler assigns the initializing values in the sequence; if the list contains fewer values than the number of elements in the array, the compiler assigns zeros to the elements that do not receive initial values from the list.

How does the C++ compiler copy the items in a linear list of initializing values into the elements of a multidimensional array? Well, the compiler fills up the elements at the higher-dimension number before the ones at the lower-dimension number. The following example explains this storage scheme.

Consider the array fMat, which has 3 rows and 2 columns. The dimension for the rows is the low-dimension number, and the dimension for the column is the high-dimension number. The element fMat[0][0] is the first array element. Therefore, the compiler stores the first initializing value in the element fMat[0][0]. Then the compiler stores the second initializing value in the element fMat[0][1]. The compiler stores the third initializing value in the element fMat[1][0] and so on. The following is the sequence of storing the initializing values in the matrix fMat:

```
fMat[0][0]
fMat[0][1]
fMat[1][0]
fMat[1][1]
fMat[2][0]
fMat[2][1]
```

You can apply the same rule to the array fCube[3][2][2] and obtain the following sequence of initialized elements:

```
fCube[0][0][0]
fCube[0][0][1]
fCube[0][1][0]
fCube[0][1][1]
fCube[1][0][0]
fCube[1][0][1]
fCube[1][1][0]
fCube[1][1][1]
fCube[2][0][0]
fCube[2][0][1]
fCube[2][1][0]
fCube[2][1][1]
```

The following are examples of initializing multidimensional arrays:

```
// example 1
double fMat[3][2] = { 1.1, 2.2, 3.3, 4.4, 5.5, 6.6
    };
// example 2
int nMat[5][2] = { 1, 2, 3, 4, 5 };
```

The code in example 1 declares the double-type two-dimensional array fMat to have 3 rows and 2 columns. This declaration also initializes all six elements with the values 1.1, 2.2, 3.3, 4.4, 5.5, and 6.6. The compiler stores these values sequentially in elements fMat[0][0], fMat[0][1], and so on. The second example declares the int-type matrix nMat to have 5 rows and 2 columns.

This declaration initializes only the first five elements
(nMat[0][0], nMat[0][1], nMat[1][0], nMat[1][1], and
nMat[2][0]) with the values 1, 2, 3, 4, and 5. Therefore, the
compiler assigns zeros to the remaining matrix elements.

The following program, ARRAY2.CPP, illustrates initializing arrays.
This program illustrates the following features:

♦ Declaring and initializing C++ arrays. The program also
  demonstrates using the number of initializing values to
  establish the number of array elements.

♦ Initializing a data member that is an array. C++ offers no
  syntax to directly initialize data members that are arrays.

The program declares and initializes two C++ arrays and an array
object. This program performs the following tasks:

♦ Displays the initial values in the array object

♦ Increments the values in the array object by using the values
  in the two C++ arrays

♦ Displays the new values in the array object

The following is the source code for the ARRAY2.CPP program:

```
// C++ program that illustrates initializing
// multidimensional matrix elements

#include <iostream.h>
#include <stdio.h>
#include <iomanip.h>
#include <math.h>

const int MAX_ROWS = 2;
const int MAX_COLS = 5;

class myMatrix
{
  public:
    myMatrix(int bUseInitArray = 1, double fInitVal
    = 0);
    double& operator()(int nRow, int nCol)
      { return m_fMatrix[nRow][nCol]; }
    void show(const char* pszMsg = "",
              const int nNumRows = MAX_ROWS,
              const int nNumCols = MAX_COLS);

  protected:
    double m_fMatrix[MAX_ROWS][MAX_COLS];
};

myMatrix::myMatrix(int bUseInitArray, double
    fInitVal)
```

(continued)

(continued)

```cpp
{
  if (bUseInitArray) {
    double fInitMat[MAX_ROWS][MAX_COLS] =
      { 1.9, 2.3, 7.6, 3.2, 6.7,
        2.9, 3.8, 8.7, 7.5, 4.5 };
    for (int i = 0; i < MAX_ROWS; i++)
      for (int j = 0; j < MAX_COLS; j++)
        m_fMatrix[i][j] = fInitMat[i][j];
  }
  else
    for (int i = 0; i < MAX_ROWS; i++)
      for (int j = 0; j < MAX_COLS; j++)
        m_fMatrix[i][j] = fInitVal;
}

void myMatrix::show(const char* pszMsg,
                    const int nNumRows,
                    const int nNumCols)
{
  char cString[10];

  cout << pszMsg << endl;
  for (int i = 0; i < nNumRows; i++) {
    for (int j = 0; j < nNumCols; j++) {
      sprintf(cString, "%3.1lf ", m_fMatrix[i][j]);
      cout << cString;
    }
    cout << endl;
  }
}

main()
{
  double fXMat[2][MAX_ROWS][MAX_COLS] =
      { // data for sub-array fMat[0][][]
        19.9, 29.3, 87.6, 43.2, 76.7,
        32.9, 43.8, 88.7, 87.5, 64.5,
        // data for sub-array fMat[1][][]
        111.9, 222.3, 777.6, 333.2, 676.7,
        222.9, 333.8, 688.7, 787.5, 484.5 };
  myMatrix Matrix;

  // show the matrix
  Matrix.show("Initial matrix is:");

  cout << endl;

  // update matrix Matrix
  for (int i = 0; i < MAX_ROWS; i++)
    for (int j = 0; j < MAX_COLS; j++)
      Matrix(i, j) = fXMat[1][i][j] /
      fXMat[0][i][j];
```

```
    // show the matrix
    Matrix.show("New matrix is:");

    return 0;
}
```

The following is the output of this program:

```
Initial matrix is:
1.9 2.3 7.6 3.2 6.7
2.9 3.8 8.7 7.5 4.5

New matrix is:
5.6 7.6 8.9 7.7 8.8
6.8 7.6 7.8 9.0 7.5
```

This program declares the constants MAX_ROWS and MAX_COLS, which define the number of rows and columns of the matrices that are used in the program. The code declares the class myMatrix, which stores and displays matrix elements. The class has a constructor that enables you to initialize the matrix in one of two ways. When the argument of the parameter bUseInitMatrix is 1 (which is the default argument) or a nonzero value, the constructor uses the local initialized C++ matrix fInitMat to provide the initializing values for the elements of the data member m_fMatrix. The constructor declares the matrix fInitMat to have MAX_ROWS rows and MAX_COLS columns. If the parameter bUseInitMatrix is 0, the constructor assigns the value of parameter fInitVal to each element in the data member m_fMatrix.

The function main() declares and initializes the three-dimensional C++ matrix fXMat. This array conceptually represents two matrices that are combined. The declaration of matrix fXMat specifies a dual matrix with MAX_ROWS rows and MAX_COLS columns. Then the function main() declares the object Matrix as an instance of class myMatrix. The way I wrote the source code, object Matrix ends up by using the default argument for the constructor of class myMatrix. Consequently, the runtime system initializes the data member m_fMatrix in object Matrix by using the matrix fInitMat. The function main() then performs the following tasks:

✦ Displays the initial elements in the object Matrix by sending it the C++ message show(). The argument for this message is the string literal "Initial matrix is:".

✦ Updates the values in the object Matrix. This task uses a nested for loop, which iterates over the elements of the matrices. Each inner loop iteration assigns the ratio fXMat[1][i][j] / fXMat[0][i][j] to the element Matrix(i, j).

✦ Displays the new values of the elements in the object Matrix by sending it the C++ message show(). The argument for this message is the string literal "New matrix is:".

Single-Dimensional Arrays

Single-dimensional arrays are the simplest kinds of arrays. You can think of this kind of array as a row or column of data. For example, you can declare a single-dimensional array to store the high temperatures of every day of the year.

Accessing single-dimensional arrays

After you declare an array, you can access its elements by using the index operator [ ]. The general syntax for accessing an element in an array is as follows:

```
arrayName[anIndex]
```

The index should be in the valid range of indices — between 0 and the number of array elements minus one.

The following are examples of accessing array elements:

```
const int MAX = 10;
double fVector[MAX];
for (int i = 0; i < MAX; i++)
   fVector[i] = double(i) * i;
for (i = MAX - 1; i >= 0; i--)
   cout << fVector[i] << "\n";
```

This code declares the constant MAX and uses that constant in declaring the double-type array fVector. Therefore, the array has elements with indices in the range of 0 to MAX - 1. The code uses the first for loop to assign values to the elements of the array fVector. The loop statement accesses the elements of array fVector by using the loop control variable i. Then the expression fVector[i] accesses the element number i in the array fVector. The source code uses the second loop to display, in descending order, the elements of the array fVector. Again, the loop statement accesses the elements of array fVector by using the loop control variable i.

Declaring single-dimensional arrays

C++ requires you to declare an array before you use it. The general syntax for declaring an array is as follows:

```
type arrayName[numberOfElements];
```

This syntax shows the following aspects:

♦ The declaration starts by stating the basic type that is associated with the array elements. You can use predefined or previously defined data types.

♦ The name of the array is followed by the number of elements. This number is enclosed in brackets. The number of array elements must be a constant (literal or symbolic) or an expression that uses constants.

All arrays in C++ have indices that start at 0. Therefore, the number of array elements is one value higher than the index of the last array element.

The following are examples of declaring arrays:

```
// example 1
int nIntArr[10];
// example 2
const int MAX = 30;
char cName[MAX];
// example 3
const int MAX_CHARS = 40;
char cString[MAX_CHARS+1];
```

The first example declares the int-type array nIntArr with 10 elements. The declaration uses the literal constant 10. Therefore, the indices for the first and last array elements are 0 and 9, respectively. The second example declares the constant MAX and uses that constant to specify the number of elements of the char-type array cName. Then the third example declares the char-type array cString. The constant expression MAX_CHARS + 1 defines the number of elements in the array cString.

Initializing single-dimensional arrays

C++ enables you to initialize some or all of the elements of an array. The general syntax for initializing an array is as follows:

```
type arrayName[numOfElems] = { value0 ,..., valueN
    };
```

You need to observe the following rules when you initialize an array:

♦ The list of initial values appears in a pair of braces and is comma-delimited. The list ends with a closing brace followed by a semicolon.

♦ The list may contain a number of initial values that are equal to or less than the number of elements in the initialized array. Otherwise, the compiler generates a compile-time error.

♦ The compiler assigns the first initializing value to the element at index 0, the second initializing value to the element at index 1, and so on.

♦ If the list contains fewer values than the number of elements in the array, the compiler assigns zeros to the elements that do not receive initial values from the list.

♦ If you omit the number of array elements, the compiler uses the number of initializing values in the list as the number of array elements.

The following are examples of initializing arrays:

```
// example 1
double fArr[5] = { 1.1, 2.2, 3.3, 4.4, 5.5 };
// example 2
int nArr[10] = { 1, 2, 3, 4, 5 };
// example 3
char cVowels[] = { 'A' , 'a', 'E', 'e', 'I', 'i',
    'O', 'o', 'U', 'u' };
```

The code in example 1 declares the double-type array fArr to have five elements. This declaration also initializes all five elements with the values 1.1, 2.2, 3.3, 4.4, and 5.5. The second example declares the int-type array nArr to have ten elements. This declaration also initializes only the first five elements with the values 1, 2, 3, 4, and 5. Therefore, the compiler assigns zeros to the elements at index 5 through 9 of the array nArr. The last example declares the char-type array cVowels and initializes the array elements with the lowercase and uppercase vowels. Because the declaration of array cVowels does not specify the number of elements, the compiler uses the number of initializing values, 10, as the number of elements in the array cVowels.

The following program, ARRAY1.CPP, shows you how to declare an initialized array of integers. This source code performs the following tasks:

♦ Declares an array of integers and initializes the array with a set of values

♦ Displays the initial elements of the array

♦ Sorts the array by using the bubble sort method

♦ Displays the elements of the sorted array

The following is the source code for the ARRAY1.CPP program:

```
/* ARRAY1.CPP

    A C++ program that illustrates
    declaring and initializing a single-dimension
    array
```

```
*/

#include <iostream.h>

main()
{
  const int MAX_ELEMS = 5;
  int nAgeArr[MAX_ELEMS] = { 41, 67, 95, 29, 55 };
  int i, j, k, nSwapBuffer;

  cout << "Initial array is : ";
  for (k = 0 ; k < MAX_ELEMS; k++)
    cout << nAgeArr[k] << " ";
  cout << "\n";

  // sort the array
  for (i = 0; i < (MAX_ELEMS - 1); i++) {
    for (j = i+1; j < MAX_ELEMS; j++) {
      if (nAgeArr[i] > nAgeArr[j]) {
        nSwapBuffer = nAgeArr[i];
        nAgeArr[i] = nAgeArr[j];
        nAgeArr[j] = nSwapBuffer;
      }
    }
  }

  cout << "Sorted array is : ";
  for (k = 0 ; k < MAX_ELEMS; k++)
    cout << nAgeArr[k] << " ";
  cout << "\n";

  return 0;
}
```

The following is a sample session with the ARRAY1.CPP program:

```
Initial array is : 41 67 95 29 55
Sorted array is : 29 41 55 67 95
```

These statements show the function main(), which declares the constant MAX_ELEMS, the int-type array nAgeArr, and the int-type variables i, j, k, and nSwapBuffer. The function declares the array nAgeArr as having MAX_ELEMS elements and initializes the array elements with the values 41, 67, 95, 29, and 55. The function performs the following tasks:

+ Displays the initial array elements on one line. This task uses a for loop to display these elements.

+ Sorts the array. This task uses nested for loops that use the control variables i and j.

+ Displays the sorted array elements on one line. This task uses a for loop to display these elements.

Part IX

Pointers

A *pointer* is a special variable that stores the address of another variable or object. Knowing the address of a variable or object enables a pointer to access the data in that variable or object.

In this part . . .

- ✔ Working with constant pointers
- ✔ Declaring pointers
- ✔ Declaring pointers in an array
- ✔ Using far pointers
- ✔ Passing arrays as function parameters
- ✔ Working with pointers to arrays
- ✔ Working with pointers to existing variables
- ✔ Using pointers to functions
- ✔ Using pointers to pointers
- ✔ Using pointers to objects
- ✔ Working with pointers to structures
- ✔ Comparing reference variables with pointers

Constant Pointers

Reference variables have a fixed association with the variables that they refer to. Furthermore, you can assign a new address to a pointer, making pointers more flexible than reference variables. C++ enables you to declare constant pointers so that the initial address they store remains fixed. In other words, the compiler generates an error if you attempt to store a new address in the constant pointer. Therefore, constant pointers and reference variables are very similar. They differ in their syntax but are otherwise functionally equivalent. The general syntax for declaring a constant pointer is as follows:

```
const type* pointerName = address;
```

The following are examples using constant pointers:

```
const char* pszName = "Namir Shammas";
int nNum = 12;
const int* pnNum = &nNum;
```

The first example is an interesting one. It declares a constant char-type pointer, pszName, and assigns it the address of a literal string. This example is typical of using constant pointers to access string literals. You can access and manipulate the string literal by using another pointer. However, while the string literal is in scope, the pointer pszName accesses its address. The second example shows the constant int-type pointer pnNum, which stores the address of the int-type variable nNum.

Declaring Pointers

As with ordinary variables, you must declare a pointer before you can use it. The general syntax for declaring a pointer is as follows:

```
// form 1
type* pointerName;
// form 2
type *pointerName;
// form 3
type * pointerName;
```

This syntax declares a pointer and states the data type that is associated with the pointer. Keep in mind that this is *not* the type of the pointer itself but the type of the data that is *accessed* by the pointer. These statements show that you can place the asterisk character (*) directly after the type that is associated with the pointer, between the data type and the pointer or directly before the name of the pointer.

The following are examples of declaring pointers:

```
int* pnCount;
char * pszName;
int *pnInt1, *pnInt2;
```

The first example declares the pointer `pnCount` as a pointer to an `int`-type variable. Then the second example declares the pointer `pszName` as a pointer to a `char`-type variable or an ASCII string. The last example declares the pointers `pnInt1` and `pnInt2` as pointers to `int`-type variables. Notice that, in the case of declaring multiple pointers, the asterisk appears before the name of each pointer.

Because pointers store the address of other items, it is imperative to *properly initialize* pointers *before* using them. If you are new to pointers, it is important to remember this rule, because your system may crash if the rule isn't followed. Check out the section "Initializing Pointers" to see how to initialize pointers.

Declaring an Array of Function Pointers

In addition to declaring individual function pointers, C++ enables you to declare an array of function pointers. Each pointer in this kind of array stores the address of a function. The general syntax for declaring an array of function pointers is as follows:

```
type
    (*pointerToFunction[numberOfPointers])(parameterList);
```

This syntax shows that declaring an array of function pointers is similar to declaring a single function pointer. The main difference is that the name of the array must be followed by the number of pointers, enclosed in brackets.

When you assign the address of a function to an element in an array or a function pointer, you must include the element's index, as shown in the following general syntax:

```
type functionName(parameterList);
type (*pointerToFunction[numElems])(parameterList);
pointerToFunction[nIndex] = functionName;
```

The general syntax for invoking a function by using its pointer is as follows:

```
(*pointerToFunction[nIndex])(argumentList)
```

The following is an example of declaring and using an array of function pointers:

```
// prototype function
void StatSearch(int* pnArray, int nNumArray,
                int nSearchVal);
void LinearSearch(int* pnArray, int nNumArray,
                  int nSearchVal);

main()
{
  int nArray[100] = { 44, 55, 66, 77, 32, 12 };
  int nCount = 6;
  int nSearchVal = nArray[1];
  // declare pointer to function
  void (*Search[2])(int*, int, int);

  // assign address of function LinearSearch to
  // pointer Search
  Search[0] = LinearSearch;
  // assign address of function StatSearch to
  // pointer Search
  Search[1] = StatSearch;
  // other statements
  // invoke LinearSearch
  (*Search[0])(nArray, nCount, nSearchVal);
  // other statements
  // invoke StatSearch
  (*Search[1])(nArray, nCount, nSearchVal);
  // other statements

  return 0;
}
```

This example declares the function main() and the prototypes of
functions StatSearch() and LinearSearch(). The function
main() declares the array of function pointers Search to have
two elements. Notice that the return type and parameter list for
this pointer match those in functions StatSearch() and
LinearSearch(). The function main first assigns the addresses
of functions LinearSearch() and StatSearch() to pointers
Search[0] and Search[1], respectively. Then the function uses
pointer Search[0] to invoke the function LinearSearch() and
pointer Search[1] to invoke the function StatSearch(). The
arguments for each invocation are the array nArray, the variable
nCount, and the variable nSearchVal.

Far Pointers

Pointers store addresses. What is important about these addresses? The operating systems DOS and Windows 3.1 use
memory segments. To save space, the pointers store only the
offset address from the start of the current memory segment. This
kind of pointer is caller a *near pointer.* C++ supports another kind
of pointer, called the *far pointer,* which stores the entire address —

both the *segment* and *offset* parts. Far pointers use more memory to store the segment and offset addresses. The general syntax for declaring near and far pointers is as follows:

```
[const] type* __near pointerName [= address];
[const] type* __far pointerName [= address];
```

The declaration of pointers creates near pointers by default. The following are examples of far and near pointers:

```
int* __far pNum1 = &nNum1;
int* __far pNum2 = &nNum2;
const myArrayClass* __far pArray;
const char* __near pszMsg = "Hello There!";
```

This code declares the far int-type pointers pNum1 and pNum2. In addition, the code shows the declaration of a far pointer to a class and a near pointer to a string.

Initializing Pointers

You must assign an address to a pointer before you can use that pointer. Moreover, the address should be valid and not one that accesses a critical location in your computer's memory; otherwise, you are playing Russian Roulette with the operating system. The results are not predictable! You can declare and initialize pointers in the same statement. The general syntax for the combined declaration and initialization is as follows:

```
// form 1
type* pointerName = address;
// form 2
type *pointerName = address;
// form 3
type * pointerName = address;
```

The address that initializes the pointer is typically either the address of an existing variable or the address of a dynamic variable.

The following are examples of declaring and initializing pointers:

```
// example 1
int nCount
int* pnCount = &nCount;
// example 2
char * pszName = new char[81];
```

The first example declares int-type variable nCount and the int-type pointer pnCount. The example also initializes this pointer by using the address of the variable nCount. The second example declares the pointer pszName as a pointer to a char-type variable and initializes it with the address of a dynamic array of characters.

You can also declare and initialize a pointer in two separate statements. Here is an example:

```
int nCount
int* pnCount;
pnCount = &nCount
```

The preceding example declares int-type variable nCount and the int-type pointer pnCount. The example then uses a separate statement to initialize this pointer by using the address of the variable nCount.

Passing Arguments by Pointer

C++ enables you to pass arguments by value, by using a pointer, or by using a reference. This section reviews passing parameters by using pointers to enumerated types, structures, and functions. When you pass the address of an argument to a function, that function can alter the value of the argument, such that the change remains in effect after the function ends executing. Thus using pointers enables you to pass multiple values back to the caller of the function. This feature solves limitation of getting one value back from a function.

Pointers to enumerated types as function parameters

You can use pointers to enumerated types as function parameters. This type of parameter serves to either pass an array of enumerators or pass a single enumerator *back* to the function caller. You can use a reference parameter to perform the same task. The general syntax for declaring a pointer to an enumerated type as a function parameter is as follows:

```
[const] type* pointerToEnumeratedType
```

Using the const keyword prevents the function from altering the values in the enumerated type. The following is an example of using pointers to an enumerated type as function parameters:

```
enum Colors { Red, Blue, Green, Yellow };
void getScreenColors(Colors* pForegroundColor, /*
    output */
                        Colors* pBackgroundColor  /*
    output */);
```

The function getScreenColors() returns the foreground and background colors to the function caller. The parameter pForegroundColor is the pointer to the foreground color, and the parameter `pBackgroundColor` is the pointer to the background color. Both parameters yield enumerators to the function caller.

Pointers to structures as function parameters

C++ enables you to use pointers to structures as function parameters. There are three typical uses for this kind of pointer:

✦ Passing a pointer to a structured variable instead of a copy of that variable eliminates the overhead of making a copy of the variable for the function to use.

✦ Passing a pointer to a structured variable enables the pointer to support two-way data flow between the function and its caller.

✦ Passing a pointer to a structure type enables the function to process an array of structures.

The general syntax for declaring a pointer to a structure as a function parameter is as follows:

`[const] type* pointerToStructure`

Using the `const` keyword prevents the function from altering the values in the structure. Omitting the `const` keyword enables the function to alter the values in the structure and to submit the update back to the caller.

The following is an example of using a pointer to a structure as a function parameter:

```
struct ScreenChars
{
  // members
};

void LoadScreen(ScreenChars* pScreen /* input */);
void SaveScreen(ScreenChars* pScreen /* output */);
void UpdateScreen(ScreenChars* pScreen /* in/out */
   );
```

This example declares the structure `ScreenChars` and the prototype of the functions `LoadScreen()`, `SaveScreen()`, and `UpdateScreen()`. All three functions have the `ScreenChars`-type pointer parameter `pScreen`. The function `LoadScreen()` uses the pointer to quickly access a `ScreenChars`-type variable. Next, the function `SaveScreen()` uses the pointer `pScreen` to output the screen's data to a `ScreenChars`-type variable. Finally, the function `UpdateScreen()` uses the pointer `pScreen` to pass screen-related data to and from the function.

The preceding example shows three functions with the same pointer declaration. However, each function uses the pointer parameter for a different pattern of data flow. The function LoadScreen() uses parameter pScreen for data input only. The function ScaveScreen() uses parameter pScreen for data output only. The function UpdateScreen() uses parameter pScreen for data input and output. By simply looking at the declaration of parameter pScreen, you cannot determine the pattern of data flow through that pointer. This weakness in C++ makes a program difficult to debug.

Pointers to functions as parameters

After understanding function pointers, you may ask whether C++ allows these pointers to be function parameters. The answer is yes! C++ enables you to declare function parameters that are pointers to other functions. This is a very powerful programming language; it allows a function to use other functions that are selected at runtime instead of compile time.

The declaration of a function pointer as a parameter uses the same syntax as the declaration of a function pointer as a variable.

The following is an example of declaring and using function pointers as function parameters:

```
// prototype function
void StatSearch(int* pnArray, int nNumArray,
                int nSearchVal);
void LinearSearch(int* pnArray, int nNumArray,
                int nSearchVal);
void SearchAndSave(int* pnArray, int nNumArray,
                int nSearchVal,
                void (*pSort)(int*, int),
                const char* pszFilename);

main()
{
  const char* pszFilename = "ARRAY.DAT";
  int nArray[100] = { 44, 55, 66, 77, 32, 12 };
  int nCount = 6;
  int nSearchVal = nArray[1];
  // declare pointer to function
  void (*Search)(int*, int, int);

  // assign address of function LinearSearch to
  // pointer Search
  Search = LinearSearch;
  // other statements
  // invoke LinearSearch and save data to a file
  SearchAndSave(nArray, nCount, nSearchVal,
                (*Search)(nArray, nCount,
    nSearchVal),
                pszFilename);
```

```
    // other statements
    // assign address of function StatSearch to
    // pointer Search
    Search = StatSearch;
    // invoke StatSearch
    SearchAndSave(nArray, nCount, nSearchVal,
                  (*Search)(nArray, nCount,
      nSearchVal),
                        pszFilename);
    // other statements

    return 0;
}
```

This example declares the function main() and the prototypes for functions StatSearch(), LinearSearch(), and Search(). The latter function has a function pointer parameter whose return type and parameter list match those of the functions LinearSearch() and StatSearch(). The function main declares the function pointer Search. Notice that the return type and parameter list for this pointer match those in the functions StatSearch() and LinearSearch(). The function main first assigns the address of function LinearSearch() to the pointer Search. Then the function main() calls function SearchAndSave() to search the array nArray by using the LinearSearch() function. The arguments for this invocation are the array nArray, the variable nCount, the variable nSearchVal, the function pointer Search, and the constant pointer pszFilename. Then the function main assigns the address of function StatSearch() to the pointer Search and calls the function SearchAndSave() a second time. The arguments for this function call match those of the first call to the function SearchAndSave().

Passing Arrays as Function Parameters

You can use pointers to arrays as function parameters. This kind of pointer enables you to pass a static or dynamic array as an argument to a function. The general syntax for declaring a pointer to an array as a function parameter is as follows:

[const] type* pointerToArray

Using the const keyword prevents the function from altering the values in the array. In other words, using this keyword makes the values in the array read-only. Omitting the const keyword enables the function to alter the values in the array argument and submit the update back to the caller. Using pointers to arrays as function parameters enables you to write functions that handle arrays of varying sizes.

The following are examples using pointers to arrays as function parameters:

```
struct myPersonnelData
{
  // members
};

void Sort(int* pnArray, int nNumberOfElements);
int LinearSearch(myPersonnelData* pData, int
    nNumberOfElements,
                    myPersonnelData searchData);
void Show(double* pfArray, int nNumElems);
```

This example shows the prototypes of the functions `Sort()`, `LinearSearch()`, and `Show()`. The function `Sort()` sorts an array of integers. Notice that the first parameter `pnArray` is the pointer to an `int`-type array. The function `LinearSearch()` then searches an array of `myPersonnelData`. Notice that the first parameter `pData` is the pointer to a `myPersonnelData`-type array. The function `Show()` displays a `double`-type array. The first parameter `pfArray` is the pointer to a `double`-type array. All the functions in the previous example include a second parameter that passes the number of elements for the function to process.

Pointers to Arrays

Pointers work well in accessing the elements of an array. This section looks at how pointers and arrays relate and how to use address arithmetic with pointers.

Array names are pointers, too!

C++, like its parent language C, regards the name of an array as a pointer to the first element in that array. So, for example, you may declare the following array:

```
char cName[30];
```

In this case, the name of the array `cName` is equivalent to the address of the first array element, `&cName[0]`. This feature gives you a useful shorthand way to write the address of the first element. Therefore, you can assign the address of the first array element to a pointer by simply using the name of the array. The following is an example of this feature:

```
int nArr[30];
int *pnArr = nArr; // same as int *pnArr =
    &nArr[0];
```

This example declares the array nArr and the pointer pnArr. The example initializes the pointer with the address of the first element in array nArr by simply assigning the name of the array to the pointer. You can replace nArr with the expression &nArr[0] to assign the same address to the pointer.

Pointer arithmetic

One of the benefits of associating a data type with a pointer is pointer arithmetic, which increments or decrements the address in the pointer. What happens when you apply the +, -, ++, and -- operators to a pointer? Does it alter the address by bytes or by the size of the item that is pointed to? The answer is that these operators increment or decrement the address of the pointers by the product of the amount of change multiplied by the data item size. The following is an example that illustrates this feature:

```
const int MAX = 4;
int nArr[MAX] = { 1, 2, 3, 4 };
int* pnArr = nArr;

cout << *pnArr << endl; // displays nArr[0];
*pnArr++;
cout << *pnArr++ << endl; // displays nArr[1];
cout << *pnArr << endl; // displays nArr[2];
```

This example assigns the address of the first element in array nArr to the pointer pnArr. The first output statement displays the value in element nArr[0]. The next statement increments the address in pointer pnArr. This pointer now points to the second element nArr[1]. The second output statement displays the value in the element nArr[1]. This statement also uses the post-increment operator ++ to increment the address in the pointer pnArr. This pointer now points to the third array element nArr[1]. The last output statement displays the value in element nArr[2].

Array element access via pointers

You can access the elements of an array by using a pointer to the array elements. The process of systematically accessing the array elements by using a pointer involves the following general steps:

1 Initialize the pointer with the first (or last) array element.

2 Use a loop to access each array element and increment (or decrement) the address in the pointer.

The general syntax for accessing an array element by using a pointer is as follows:

```
type* pointerName = arrayName;
*(pointerName + index) is equivalent to
    arrayName[index]
*(pointerName + index) is equivalent to
    pointerName[index]
```

Notice that C++ offers two forms for accessing the elements of an array by using a pointer (and there are two forms for using the pointer). The following is an example of accessing a single-dimensional array by using a pointer:

```
const int MAX = 100;
double fArr[MAX];
double* pfArr = fArr;

for (int i = 0; i < MAX; i++)
  *(pfArr + i) = double(i * i - 3 * i + 3);

for (int i = 0; i < MAX; i++)
  pfArr[i] += 1.2 * pfArr[i] + 3.4;
```

This example declares the double-type array fArr and the double-type pointer pfArr. The example initializes the pointer with the address of the first array element. Then the example uses the first for loop to initialize the array elements. The loop uses the pointer pfArr to access the array element. Notice that the expression *(pfArr + i) is equivalent to fArr[i]. The example uses the second for loop to further manipulate the values in the array. Notice that this loop's statement uses the expression pfArr[i] instead of fArr[i] to access the array elements.

Pointers to Existing Variables

You can store the address of an existing variable in a pointer that has the same associated type. The general syntax for declaring a pointer and initializing it with the address of an existing variable is as follows:

```
type variableName [= initialValue];
type* pointerName = &variableName;
```

This syntax uses the address-of operator & to obtain the address of the variable and assign it to the pointer. The following is an example:

```
int nCount = 0;
int* pnCount = &nCount;
```

This example declares and initializes the int-type variable nCount and declares and initializes the int-type pointer pnCount. The initialization step stores the address of variable nCount in the pointer pnCount.

C++ enables you to defer initializing a pointer by assigning it the address of a variable in a statement that is separate from the declaration of the pointer.

Remember: You must properly initialize pointers before using them or your system will crash.

The general syntax for assigning an address to a pointer is as follows:

```
type variableName;
type* pointerName;
// statements
pointerName = &variableName;
```

The address assignment uses the address-of operator &. The following is an example:

```
int nCount;
int* pnCount;

cin >> nCount;
pnCount = &nCount;
```

This example declares the int-type variable nCount and the int-type pointer pnCount. The example assigns a value to variable nCount from the input stream and then stores the address of variable nCount in the pointer pnCount.

Pointers to Functions

C++, like C, enables you to declare and use pointers to functions. These pointers store the address of a function (that is, the location of the first executable statement). You can use pointers to functions to invoke the functions. The general syntax for declaring a pointer to a function is as follows:

```
type (*pointerToFunction)(parameterList) [=
    functionAddress];
```

When you initialize a pointer to a function, you must use the name of a function that has the same return type and parameter list. The general syntax for this kind of assignment is as follows:

```
type functionName(parameterList);
type (*pointerToFunction)(parameterList);
pointerToFunction = functionName;
```

The general syntax for invoking a function by using its pointer is as follows:

```
(*pointerToFunction)(argumentList)
```

The following is an example of declaring and using a pointer to functions:

```
// prototype function
int LinearSearch(int* pnArray, int nNumArray,
                 int nSearchVal);
int StatSearch(int* pnArray, int nNumArray,
               int nSearchVal);

main()
{
  int nArray[100] = { 44, 55, 66, 77, 32, 12 };
  int nCount = 6;
  int nSearchVal = nArray[1];
  // declare pointer to function
  int (*Search)(int*, int , int);

  // assign address of function LinearSearch to
  // pointer Search
  Search = LinearSearch;
  // other statements
  // invoke LinearSearch
  (*Search)(nArray, nCount, nSearchVal);
  // other statements
  // assign address of function StatSearch to
  // pointer Search
  Search = StatSearch;
  // other statements
  // invoke StatSearch
  (*Search)(nArray, nCount, nSearchVal);
  // other statements

  return 0;
}
```

This example declares the functions StatSearch() and LinearSearch(). The function main() declares the function pointer Search. Notice that the return type and parameter list for this pointer match those in the functions StatSearch() and LinearSearch(). The function main first assigns the address of function LinearSearch() to pointer Search and then uses that pointer to invoke the function LinearSearch(). The arguments for this invocation are the array nArray, the variable nCount, and the variable nSearchVal. These arguments match the parameter list of the function pointer (and the function that it points to). The function main then assigns the address of function StatSearch() to pointer Search and then uses that pointer to invoke the function StatSearch(). The arguments for this invocation are the array nArray, the variable nCount, and the variable nSearchVal.

Pointers to Objects

C++ enables you to declare pointers to classes to access the various instances of that class. The declaration and address assignment of a pointer to a class is just like that of simple variables.

The following is an example using a pointer to a class:

```
#include <iostream.h>

class myComplex
{
 public:
  myComplex()
    { setComplex(0, 0); }
  void setComplex(double fReal, double fImag)
    {
     m_fReal = fReal;
     m_fImag = fImag;
    }
  double getReal()
    { return m_fReal; }
  double getImag()
    { return m_fImag; }

 protected:
  double m_fReal;
  double m_fImag;
};

main()
{
 myComplex ComplexObj;
 myComplex* pComplex = &ComplexObj;

 pComplex->setComplex(1.2, 3.4);
 cout << "Complex number is "
     << pComplex->getReal()
     << " + i "
     << pComplex->getImag();
 return 0;
}
```

This example declares the class myComplex with protected and public members. The class declares the double-type protected data members m_fReal and m_fImag to store the real and imaginary parts of a complex number. Then the class declares a public constructor and the member functions setComplex, getReal, and getImag. The function main() declares the object ComplexObj as an instance of the class myComplex. This function also declares the pointer pComplex as a pointer to the object ComplexObj. Then the function main assigns a new complex value by sending the C++ message setComplex to the object, using the pointer pComplex. Similarly, the function main displays the value in the object `Complex` by sending the C++ messages `getReal` and `getImag` to that object, again using the pointer `pComplex`.

Pointers to Pointers

C++ enables you to declare a pointer to another pointer. This kind of advanced use of pointers works well, for example, in managing dynamic two-dimensional arrays. One pointer accesses the rows of this kind of dynamic array, while the other one accesses the columns in that row. The general syntax for declaring a pointer to a pointer is as follows:

```
type** pointerToPointerName;
```

The following are examples for declaring, initializing, and using pointers to pointers:

```
int nNum = 1;
int* pnNum = &nNum;
int** ppnNum = &pnNum;
cout << nNum << "\n"; // displays 1 using the
     variable nNum
cout << *pnNum << "\n"; // displays 1 using the
     pointer pnNum
cout << **ppnNum << "\n"; // displays 1
                          // using the pointer-to-
                          // pointer ppnNum
```

This example declares the `int`-type variable `nNum`, the `int`-type pointer `pnNum`, and the `int`-type pointer-to-pointer `ppnNum`. The declarations in the example also include initializations. This example contains three output statements that display the value in variable `nNum` by using that variable, the pointer `pnNum`, and the pointer-to-pointer `ppnNum`.

Pointers to Structures

You can declare pointers to structures and access the data members of these structures by using the pointers. C++ enables you to use the pointer access operator `->`. The general syntax for declaring a pointer a structured variable is the same as the one for ordinary variables.

The following is an example of declaring a pointer to a structured variable and using it to access the data members of that structure:

```
struct myComplex
{
 double m_fReal;
 double m_fImag;
};

main()
{
 myComplex ComplexVar = { 1.0, 2.0 };
 myComplex* pComplex = &ComplexVar;

 cout << "Complex number = "
    << pComplex->m_fReal
    << " + i "
    << pComplex->m_fImag;

 return 0;
};
```

This example declares the structure myComplex with its double-type data members m_fReal and m_fImag. The function main() declares and initializes the structured variable ComplexVar. This function also declares the myComplex-type pointer pComplex and initializes it by using the address of the variable ComplexVar. The function then displays the values of the data members in variable ComplexVar by using the pointer pComplex. Notice that the output statement uses the operator -> to access the data members m_fReal and m_fImag of the structured variable.

Reference Variables versus Pointers

Reference variables and pointers are somewhat similar but yet different. The differences are as follows:

✦ A reference variable must be initialized when declared. By contrast, you can declare a pointer but not initialize it.

✦ You can assign the address of a variable to a pointer anywhere in the statements of a function. However, you cannot assign a new reference to a variable to a reference variable.

✦ Using the pointer to access the data of its associated variable requires the indirection operator *. By contrast, a reference variable does not require the indirection operator *, because it is an alias to the referenced variable.

Like pointers, reference variables become aliases to the variables they are connected with. You can alter the value of the referenced variable by using the associated reference variable (just as you can with a pointer that stores the address of that variable).

Part X

Functions and Arguments

Functions are to C++ programs as the moving parts are to a machine. Functions enable a program to interact with you and perform the tasks needed. Using functions enables you to divide the program's main tasks into smaller tasks. This approach makes it easier to write and update the source code for a program. Part X looks at the various aspects of functions, including arguments, and the information a function receives from other functions.

In this part . . .

✔ **Working with arguments**

✔ **Using functions**

Arguments

Arguments are values passed to parameters of a function. These values supply the function with needed information. For example, you can supply a name of a person to a function that searches in a phone book database.

Default arguments

Have you ever written a function and supplied most of its parameters with the same arguments for different function calls? If you have, you may have felt frustrated feeding the function call with the same values for some of the arguments. The good news is that C++ enables you to assign default arguments for parameters. The compiler uses these arguments if you do not include them when you call a function. The syntax for the default argument, which resembles the initialization of a variable, is as follows:

dataType parameterName = initialValue

C++ requires you to observe the following rules for declaring and using default arguments:

✦ When you assign a default argument to a parameter, you must assign default arguments to all subsequent parameters.

✦ You may assign default arguments to any or all parameters as long as you obey the previous rule.

✦ The default arguments feature divides the parameter list of a function into two parts. The first part contains parameters with no default arguments. (This list may be empty if you assign default arguments to all parameters.) The second part contains parameters with default arguments.

✦ To use a default argument of a parameter, omit the argument for that parameter in a function call.

✦ If you use a default argument for a parameter, you must use the default arguments for all subsequent parameters. In other words, you cannot pick and choose the default arguments, because the compiler is unable to discern which argument goes to which parameter.

The following is an example of a function with default arguments. Consider the declaration of the function myPower().

```
double myPower(double fBase,
               double fExponent = 2.0,
               double fErrorCode = -1.0e+30);
```

This code declares the function `myPower()` with the three `double`-type parameters `fBase`, `fExponent`, and `fErrorCode`. The function assigns the default arguments of 2 and –1.0e+30 to the parameters `fExponent` and `fErrorCode`, respectively. Therefore, you can use the function `myPower()` as follows:

```
double fX = 12.5;
double fXSquared = myPower(fX);
double fXCubed = myPower(fX, 3);
double fXFourth = myPower(fX, 4, -1.0e+40);
```

The first call to the function `myPower()` has only one argument. The compiler resolves this call by using the default arguments for parameters `fExponent` and `fErrorCode`. Therefore, the function `myPower()` returns squares when using the default argument for parameter `fExponent`. The second call to function `myPower()` has two arguments. The compiler resolves this call by using the default argument for the parameter `fErrorCode`. The last call to function `myPower()` has three arguments — one for each of the three parameters of the function.

Arrange the default arguments in the order of increasing likelihood of using their default values.

Passing arguments by reference

C++ enables you to pass arguments for reference parameters. The functions can change the value of these arguments beyond the function calls, because the reference parameters act as aliases to their arguments.

You can use references to enumerated types as function parameters to either establish a two-way flow of data between a function and its caller or to simply return enumerators to the function caller. The following is an example of using references to enumerated types as function parameters:

```
enum weekDay { Sunday, Monday, Tuesday, Wednesday,
   Thursday,
 Friday, Saturday };
void next(weekday& eDay /* input and output */);
void nextAndPrevious(weekDay eToday, /* input */
 weekday& eTomorrow, /* output */
 weekDay& eYesterday /* output */);
```

This example shows the enumerated type `weekDay` and the declarations of functions `next()` and `nextAndPrevious()`. The function `next()` has the reference enumerated type parameter `eDay`, which passes the current day to the function and returns the next day to the function caller. The function `nextAndPrevious()` has three enumerated type parameters. The first parameter, `eToday`, passes a day enumerator to the function. The reference parameters `eTomorrow` and `eYesterday` pass the enumerators to the next and previous days, respectively, to the caller of the function.

As previously mentioned, you can use references to structures as function parameters to either establish a two-way flow of data between a function or its caller or to return information to the function caller. The following is an example using references to structures as function parameters:

```
struct intRange
{
  int m_nMinVal;
  int m_nMaxVal;
  int m_nTheVal;
  int m_nErrorCode;
};
void setRange(int nMin, int nMax, intRange& anInt);
void setVal(int nNum, intRange& anInt);
```

This example declares the structure `intRange` to support a range of integers. The example also declares the prototypes for the functions `setRange()` and `setVal()`. These functions have the reference parameter `anInt`, which supports two-way data flow between the function and its caller. The function `setRange` assigns the values of the parameters `nMin` and `nMax` to the data members `m_nMinVal` and `m_nMaxVal` of the parameter `anInt`. Then the function `setVal()` assigns the value of the parameter `nNum` to the data member `m_nTheVal` of parameter `anInt`, If that value lies in the range that is defined by data members `m_nMinVal` and `m_nMaxVal`. The function `setVal()` also stores the error code of its operation in the data member `m_nErrorCode`.

Strings as arguments

C++ enables you to declare string parameters as pointers to characters or constant pointers to characters. The general syntax for declaring string parameters in functions is as follows:

```
[const] char* parameterName [= "defaultArgument"]
```

The following are examples for declaring string parameters in functions:

```
void orderCharacters(char* pszString);
int myStringLength(const char* pszString);
```

This example declares the functions `orderCharacters()` and `myStringLength()`. The function `orderCharacters()` has a `char*`-type parameter that points to a string variable. Notice that the name of the function suggests that its task is to order the characters of the string arguments. The function `myStringLength()` has a `const char*`-type parameter that points to a string variable. The name of this function suggests that it does not alter the contents of the string arguments.

You can also declare function parameters that are arrays of strings. The general syntax for these parameters is as follows:

```
[const] char* parameterName[]
```

The following is an example of a function that has a parameter which is an array of strings:

```
void showStrings(char* pszArrayOfSrings[], int
    nNumberOfElements);
```

This example declares the function `showStrings()`, which displays the strings that are accessed by the parameter `pszArrayOfSrings`. This parameter is an array of strings. The parameter `nNumberOfElements` specifies the number of array elements to display.

Functions

A C++ program is made up of a collection of functions (and member functions, which are special kinds of functions that are encapsulated in classes). Program execution starts with the function `main()`. Functions perform tasks and return values. These tasks cover every aspect of programming, such as screen output, tracking the mouse, reading from files, sending data to a modem, drawing graphics, and working with database, to name just a few.

Exiting functions

The `return` statement enables the program flow to exit a function. Simple non-`void` functions typically make the `return` statement the last statement. Therefore, exiting the function at the last statement makes sense. However, when you write a nontrivial function that checks its arguments and verifies other conditions, things may be more complicated. In these cases, the function may not be able to proceed normally due to illegal arguments or critical conditions. The solution for these cases is to have the function use additional `return` statements to support an early exit. Typically, such a function returns an error code either by using the function's return value or by using a reference parameter. Programmers typically prefer using the function's return value as an error flag.

There are other cases where the function does not need to proceed with the remaining statements, because specific arguments lead to results that require little computational effort.

In the case of a `void` function, you can use a `return` statement (with no expression following the `return` keyword) to support an early exit from that function. Again, in the case of an error, the `void` function should indicate the early exit by altering the value of a reference parameter.

Inline functions

Using functions enables you to modularize the source code of an application or a library. Each function should perform a specific task. However, using functions generates overhead code. This overhead consists of calls to the function, passing the arguments to the function, and returning the function's result. In the case of single-statement functions that are frequently called by other functions, you can speed program execution (perhaps at the cost of program size) by declaring these function as inline functions. An *inline function* looks like an ordinary function except that the compiler replaces the calls to that inline function with its statement. The compiler also replaces the function's parameters with its arguments. The general syntax for declaring an inline function is as follows:

```
inline returnType functionName(parameterList)
{
   return expression;
}
```

The declaration of an inline function must begin with the keyword `inline`. An inline function should have a single `return` statement. If you place declarations and other statements, your C++ compiler *may* elect (depending on the compiler's make and version) to simply treat the inline function as a noninline function. In other words, don't expect a C++ compiler to replace a 100-statement inline function with 100 statements!

The following is an example of an inline function:

```
inline long square(int nNum)
{
 return nNum * nNum;
}

main()
{
 int N = 3;
 cout << square(N) << "\n";
return 0;
}
```

This code declares the inline function square(), which returns the square of the int-type parameter nNum. When the function main() calls the function square(), the compiler substitutes the function call with the expression N * N. In other words, the compiler replaces the function call with the function's statement and replaces the function's parameters with the function's arguments.

Overloading

Function overloading is a programming feature that enables you to declare functions that have the same name but different parameter lists. Consider the following prototypes:

```
double myPowerDbl(double fBase, double fExponent);
double myPowerInt(double fBase, int nExponent);
double myPowerDblErr(double fBase, double
    fExponent,
double fErrorCode);
double myPowerIntEr(double fBase, int nExponent,
double fErrorCode);
```

These functions essentially perform the same task of calculating the result of raising a number to a power. The name of each function indicates what it does and hints at the client data type. For example the function myPowerDbl() suggests that it returns the power of double-type numbers. C++ enables you to use the same function name to declare and define different versions of a function. This feature is called *function overloading.* C++ requires you to observe the following rules when declaring overloaded functions:

✦ Each version of the overloaded function must have a different function *signature.* The signature of a function is defined by the number of parameters and their data types. This signature does not include its return type, because C++ enables you to ignore the return type in a statement. The signature of a function does include the sequence of parameters that have different data types.

✦ If the function has parameters with default arguments, the compiler does not include these parameters as part of the function's signature.

The following example describes how to use overloading with the preceding prototypes (and obey the first rule):

```
double myPower(double fBase, double fExponent);
double myPower(double fBase, int nExponent);
double myPower(double fBase, double fExponent,
double fErrorCode);
double myPower(double fBase, int nExponent,
double fErrorCode);
```

This code declares four versions of the overloaded function myPower(). The signatures of the overloaded functions, in the order of their declaration, are (double, double), (double, int), (double, double, double), and (double, int, double). Because each of these four signatures is unique, the compiler does not generate an error.

What about the second rule? The following is another set of myPower() functions that violate that rule:

```
// error! Functions have the same signatures
double myPower(double fBase, double fExponent =
    2.0);
double myPower(double fBase, int nExponent = 2);
double myPower(double fBase, double fExponent = 2,
double fErrorCode = -1.0E+30);
double myPower(double fBase, int nExponent = 2,
double fErrorCode = -1.0E+30);
```

These versions of the overloaded functions have the same signature, namely (double). The compiler raises an error, because it cannot resolve the call to function myPower() when you use the default arguments.

Don't abuse the function overloading feature by using the same name with many functions. This overuse makes your source code harder to read. You can instead create template functions to perform similar tasks on different data types. For example, you can write a template function as a generic add function that you can use with all different data types, such as add(int, int), add(float, float), and so on.

Parameters of functions

When you use or invoke (or, as programmers say, *call*) a function — that is, tell the function to execute its statements and perform its task — the most common and appropriate way to pass information to the function is by using the function's *parameters*.

You can think of a parameter as a variable that gets its information (is initialized) by the calling function. When you call the function, you specify the actual value of the parameter. This piece of data that you pass to the function by means of the parameter is called an *argument*. The parameter list that appears in the function declaration merely specifies what *kind* of information the function expects from its caller; parameters are really just placeholders for data. The data type of the parameter and the argument should be the same or compatible. For example, if a parameter has the int data type, the argument may be a variable that also has the int type.

The general syntax for the parameter list that appears in the function declaration is as follows:

```
dataType1[*|&] parameter1, dataType2[*|&]
    parameter2, ...
```

Notice that, in the preceding code, you must define the type and name of each parameter separately. The name of a parameter must obey the naming rules that appear in Part I. C++ does not enable you to group parameters that have the same data types. Instead, the language syntax insists that you declare each parameter with its own data type. The symbol * declares a parameter that is a pointer, whereas the symbol & declares a parameter that is a reference.

The following is an example of a function with a parameter:

```
int showAndGetNextInt(int nNumber)
{
  // increase value of parameter by 1
  nNumber++;
  cout << nNumber;
  return nNumber;
}
```

Try looking at the preceding function piece by piece:

+ The function has the int return type.

+ The function has the name showAndGetNextInt.

+ The function has the int-type parameter nNumber.

+ The statement nNumber++; adds 1 to the value in parameter nNumber. You can't get that original value back unless you stored it in another variable or you return and subtract 1 from the current value. However, the argument for parameter nNumber is still available in the calling function.

+ The statement cout << nNumber; displays the new value in parameter nNumber.

+ The statement return nNumber; returns the new value in parameter nNumber to the caller.

So how do you use the function showAndGetNextInt()? The following is source code in which the function main() calls this new function:

```
main()
{
  int nCustomerNumber = 0;
```

(continued)

(continued)

```
// display 1 and assign 1 to
// the variable nCustomerNumber
nCustomerNumber =
   showAndGetNextInt(nCustomerNumber);

// display 2 and assign 2 to
// the variable nCustomerNumber
nCustomerNumber =
   showAndGetNextInt(nCustomerNumber);

// display 3 and assign 3 to
// the variable nCustomerNumber
nCustomerNumber =
   showAndGetNextInt(nCustomerNumber);

return 0;
}
```

The function `main()` performs the following tasks:

✦ Declares the `int`-type variable `nCustomerNumber` and initializes it with the value 0.

✦ Calls the function `showAndGetNextInt()`. The function `main()` looks at the current value of the variable `nCustomerNumber` (which is 0) and makes that value the argument that it passes to the function `showAndGetNextInt()` by means of the parameter `nNumber`. Now, `main()` isn't passing `nCustomerNumber` to the other function; `main()` is simply making `nNumber` equal to `nCustomerNumber`.

Then the function `showAndGetNextInt()` takes the value 0 and returns the result of 1, stored in the parameter `nNumber`, to the function `main()`. At this point, `nCustomerNumber` hasn't changed; its value is still 0, because only the value of the parameter `nNumber` has been manipulated so far.

✦ Alters the value in variable `nCustomerNumber` by explicitly assigning the result of calling the function `showAndGetNextInt()` to that variable.

✦ Repeats the preceding tasks twice, increasing the value in variable `nCustomerNumber` from 1 to 2 (after the second call to function `showAndGetNextInt()`) and then from 2 to 3 (after the third call to function `showAndGetNextInt()`).

Therefore, each statement that calls function `showAndGetNextInt()` increases the value in the variable `nCustomerNumber` by 1. When the program reaches its end, the variable `nCustomerNumber` stores the integer 3.

Prototyping functions

Like most other language compilers, the C++ compiler sequentially digests declarations and statements as it comes across them. But what happens if the compiler encounters a statement that calls a function that is not yet defined? Consider the following program. What happens if the functions square() and cube() appear after the function main(), as the source code shows?

```
/*
 An incorrect C++ program that illustrates
 the importance of the order of declaring functions
*/
#include <iostream.h>
main()
{
 double X;
 cout << "Enter a number : ";
 cin >> X;
 cout << "The squared value of your input is "
 << square(X) << "\n";
 cout << "The cubed value of your input is "
 << cube(X) << "\n";
 return 0;
}
double square(double x)
{
 return x * x;
}
double cube(double x)
{
 return x * x * x;
}
```

The C++ compiler has a problem when it reaches the statements where function main() calls functions square() and cube(). The compiler displays an error message indicating that it doesn't know what the functions square() and cube() are supposed to be.

The answer to this problem is called *function prototyping.* This term simply means *declaring* a function (that is, telling the compiler that the function exists farther down in the source code) before you *define* it (that is, tell the compiler about the function in more detail). A function prototype has the following general syntax:

returnType functionName([optionalParameterList]);

The function prototype is similar to the function heading part of the syntax for declaring a function except that it ends with a semicolon instead of the function body. A function prototype need not show the names of the parameters — only their types. Function prototyping performs the following tasks:

✦ It informs the C++ compiler of an upcoming function that is to be defined (that is, completely implemented) later in the source code file.

✦ It tells the compiler about the parameters of the prototyped function. This information empowers the compiler to determine whether the prototyped function is being called with the correct number and type of arguments. Notice that the number of arguments matches the number of parameters and the types of arguments match those of the parameter.

Thus prototyping functions enable you to list the functions at the beginning of the source code and then define them farther down in the code. The advantage here is that you don't have to worry about the exact sequence of implementing these functions. Moreover, you can call these functions before you define them, because the compiler knows about these functions from the prototype information.

Applying function prototyping to the previous code example yields the next one, which compiles and runs correctly:

```
/*
 A correct C++ program that illustrates
 function prototyping
*/
#include <iostream.h>
// declare the function prototypes
double square(double x);
double cube(double x);
main()
{
  double X;
  cout << "Enter a number : ";
  cin >> X;
  cout << "The squared value of your input is "
  << square(X) << "\n";
  cout << "The cubed value of your input is "
  << cube(X) << "\n";
  return 0;
}
double square(double x)
{
  return x * x;
}
double cube(double x)
{
  return x * x * x;
}
```

Recursion

Recursion is a method in which a function obtains its result by calling itself. The recursive call passes different arguments and must reach a limit or condition where the function stops calling itself. These two rules prevent a recursive function from indefinitely calling itself. Conceptually, recursion is a form of iteration that does not use the formal fixed or conditional loop. Many algorithms (such as calculating factorials and performing Quick sort) can be implemented by using either recursive functions or straightforward loops. Some algorithms are easier to implement by using recursion. An example is the algorithm for parsing and evaluating mathematical expressions. This is true because an expression may contain smaller expressions. In this case, recursion offers the best solution.

The following is an example of a recursive function:

```
double recFactorial(int nNum)
{
  if (nNum > 1) {
    return nNum * recFactorial(nNum - 1);
  }
  else
    return 1.0;
}
```

The recursive function `recFactorial()` implements the recursive algorithm for calculating a factorial. This function has the return type `double` and the single `int`-type parameter `nNum`. The function uses an `if` statement to determine whether the argument for parameter `nNum` exceeds 1. If this condition is true, the function makes the recursive call to itself. The recursive call appears in the expression `nNum * recFactorial (nNum - 1)`. By contrast, if the tested condition is false, the function `factorial()` just returns 1. This part of the function provides the response that is needed to end the recursive function calls.

Syntax

Declaring a function tells the compiler about its heading, parameters, and its statements. To declare a function in C++, use the following general syntax:

```
returnType functionName([optionalParameterList])
{
  declarations and statements
  return aValue;
}
```

This syntax shows the following components of a function:

◆ `returnType` represents the name of a predefined or user-defined data type. If the return type of a function is `void`, you are telling the compiler that the function returns nothing — the function returns no data. Functions with the `void` return type simply perform tasks. If you omit the return type, the C++ compiler automatically uses the predefined `int` data type (representing integers).

◆ `functionName` represents what you want to name your function. This name should be reasonably short and descriptive of what the function does. For example, if a function adds numbers, you can call it something like `addNumbers` or `addNums`. The name cannot be a reserved C++ word (such as `switch` and `else`) or contain bizarre characters.

◆ `optionalParameterList` represents an optional list of parameters that supply the function with data. The function uses this data to perform its task and respond appropriately. This list separates the parameters by using commas; it doesn't matter how many parameters the function has. If the function has no parameters, it uses either empty parentheses or the keyword `void` inside the parentheses. The compiler treats both forms the same way. A good example of a function with no parameters is the familiar function `main()`, which appears in every code example in this book. The function `main()` has no parameters and uses the empty parentheses syntax form.

◆ The opening and closing braces — { } — contain the function's declarations and statements. These declarations and statements make up the *function body*.

◆ The `declarations and statements` inside the function body declare constants and variables that are *local* (that is, strictly owned and operated by the function) to the function. A local variable or constant is defined within the function only. You can have a local variable X and then a global variable X, and they don't mean the same thing — they don't share an address. The local variable appears and is used within the execution of the function. The statements can perform any legal operation, including making calculations, displaying output to the screen, reading input from the keyboard, and even calling other functions.

◆ The `return` statement exits the function and yields a result. Every function, except a `void` function, must have at least one `return` statement. The data type of the resulting value and the `returnType` part must be the same or at least compatible.

The following are two examples of functions:

```
void Greet()
{
 cout << "Hello World!\n"
}
```

The following reviews each part of the preceding function:

+ The return type is void.

+ The function name is Greet.

+ No parameters are in the function Greet().

+ The function has no declarations inside it and contains the single statement cout << "Hello world!\n" (the cout << part represents output to the screen).

+ The function returns no value.

The second example of a function is as follows:

```
double sqr(double x)
{
 return x * x
}
```

The following items describe each part of the preceding function:

+ The return type is double.

+ The function name is sqr.

+ The function has one parameter: double x.

+ The function declares nothing and has the single statement return x * x.

+ The function returns the squared value of parameter x.

Void functions

C++ uses the special type void to indicate that the function does not return a type. Consequently, using return statements in a void function only supports an early exit from the function. The following are examples of void functions:

```
void newLine()
{
 cout << "\n";
}
void showChar(const char* pszMsg, char c)
{
 cout << pszMsg << c << "\n";
}
```

(continued)

(continued)

```
void showInt(const char* pszMsg, int nNum)
{
  cout << pszMsg << nNum << "\n";
}
```

Notice that functions newLine(), showChar(), and showInt() have the void return type. The function newLine(), which has no parameters, simply emits a new line character. The function showChar() displays some text followed by the value of the char-type parameter. Likewise, the function showInt() displays some text followed by the value of the int-type parameter.

Part XI

Strings

C++, like its parent language C, does not have a predefined string type. C++ regards a string as an array of characters that ends with the null character. The ANSI C++ committee is working on a standard string class. Until the definition of such a class is finalized, you may find C++ compiler vendors offering you their own versions of a string class. Whether or not a string class is available to you, it is still good to understand the C string functions, because they are the building blocks for string classes.

In this part . . .

- ✔ Learning about the STRING.H library
- ✔ Comparing strings
- ✔ Concatenating strings
- ✔ Converting strings
- ✔ Copying strings
- ✔ Finding characters
- ✔ Finding substrings
- ✔ Getting the length of a string
- ✔ Initializing strings
- ✔ Reversing strings

About the STRING.H Library

The C string library offers you basic functions that manipulate *ASCIIZ* strings (also called *null-terminated* strings). If you are not a C programmer, it is important for you to understand these functions, because they enable you to carry out basic string operations without relying on a particular C++ class. Moreover, you may want to use these functions to create your own version of a string class. While the ANSI C++ committee is working on a standard string class, you may want to craft your own version to incorporate special features that meet your programming needs.

The STRING.H header file declares a rich set of functions that manipulate ASCIIZ strings. These strings must end with the null character (that is `'\0'`). The string functions use this null character to detect the end of the string. The following sections present the most relevant string-manipulating functions and show how you can encapsulate them in classes. I use different versions of the class `miniString` in the next sections.

Comparing Strings

The STRING.H header file declares the functions `strcmp()`, `stricmp()`, `strncmp()`, and `strnicmp()` to compare strings by using ASCII table values.

Strcmp function

The function `strcmp()` performs a case-sensitive comparison between two ASCIIZ strings. The declaration of the function `strcmp` is as follows:

```
int strcmp(const char *string1, const char
   *string2);
```

The parameters `string1` and `string2` are the strings that the function compares. The function returns the following values to indicate the relationships between the string parameters:

✦ A negative value indicates that `string1` is less than `string2`.

✦ A zero value indicates that `string1` is identical to `string2`.

✦ A positive value indicates that `string1` is greater than `string2`.

The following is an example using the function `strcmp()`:

```
char cString1[] = "Class";
char cString2[] = "CLASS";
cout << "Strings are ";
if (!strcmp(cString1, cString2))
  cout << "equal\n";
else
  cout << "not equal\n";
```

This example displays the text `Strings are not equal`, because the function `strcmp()` returns a nonzero value.

Stricmp function

The function `stricmp()` performs a case-insensitive comparison between two strings. The declaration of the function `stricmp()` is as follows:

```
int stricmp(const char *string1, const char
  *string2);
```

The parameters of function `stricmp()` are identical to those of the function `strcmp()`. The function performs a case-insensitive comparison between the two strings and returns values that indicate how these strings compare. The results of the function `stricmp()` are as follows:

✦ A negative value indicates that `string1` is less than `string2` (regardless of character case).

✦ A zero value indicates that `string1` is identical to `string2` (regardless of character case).

✦ A positive value indicates that `string1` is greater than `string2` (regardless of character case).

The following is an example using the function `stricmp()`:

```
char cString1[] = "Class";
char cString2[] = "CLASS";
cout << "Strings are ";
if (!stricmp(cString1, cString2))
  cout << "equal\n";
else
  cout << "not equal\n";
```

This example displays the text `Strings are not equal`, because the function `stricmp()` returns a value (because the two strings have the same characters, regardless of character case).

Strncmp function

The function `strncmp()` enables you to compare a fixed number of characters in two strings. The comparison is case-sensitive. The declaration of the function `strncmp()` is as follows:

```
int strncmp(const char *string1, const char *string2,
size_t count);
```

The parameters `string1` and `string2` are the strings that the function compares. The parameter `count` is the number of characters that are compared. The function `strncmp()` compares, at most, the first `count` characters of `string1` and `string2` and returns a value indicating the relationship between the substrings. This value has the same meaning as in the function `strcmp()`. The type `size_t` is a flexible integer type, which the compiler determines when it compiles your program.

The following is an example using the function `strncmp()`:

```
char cString1[] = "Class";
char cString2[] = "CLASS";
cout << "Substrings are ";
if (!strncmp(cString1, cString2, 1))
   cout << "equal\n";
else
   cout << "not equal\n";
```

This example displays the text Substrings are equal, because the function `strncmp()` returns a zero value — the function compares the first character in both strings.

Strnicmp function

The function `strnicmp()` compares a fixed number of characters in two strings. The comparison is case-insensitive. The declaration of the function `strnicmp()` is as follows:

```
int strnicmp(const char *string1, const char
    *string2,
size_t count);
```

The parameters of function `strnicmp()` are the same as those in the function `strncmp()`. The function `strnicmp()` returns the same kind of results as the function `strncmp()`.

The following is an example using the function `strnicmp()`:

```
char cString1[] = "Class";
char cString2[] = "CLASS";
cout << "Substrings are ";
if (!strnicmp(cString1, cString2, 3))
   cout << "equal\n";
else
   cout << "not equal\n";
```

This example displays the text Substrings are equal, because the function strnicmp() returns a zero value — the function compares the first three characters in each string. These characters match each other.

Concatenating Strings

The STRING.H header file declares the functions strcat() and strncat(), which concatenate strings. The function strcat() concatenates all of the characters of a string to another. By contrast, the function strncat() concatenates a specified number of characters to another string.

Strcat function

The declaration of function strcat() is as follows:

```
char *strcat(char *string1, const char *string2);
```

The parameter string1 is the destination string, and the parameter string2 is the source string. Notice that the function strcat() appends string2 to string1, terminates the resulting string with a null character and then returns a pointer to the start of the concatenated string. The function strcat() works with ASCIIZ strings and performs no overflow checking when it copies or appends strings.

The following is an example using the function strcat():

```
char cString1[80] = "Hello ";
char cString2[20] = "World!";
strcat(cString1, cString2);
cout << cString1 << "\n"; // displays Hello World!
```

This example declares and initializes the two ASCIIZ string variables cString1 and cString2. The example then uses the function strcat() to append the characters of string variable cString2 to the variable cString1. The output statement displays the characters Hello World!

Strncat function

The declaration of the function strncat() is as follows:

```
char *strncat(char *string1, const char *string2,
    size_t count);
```

The parameter string1 is the destination string, and the parameter string2 is the source string. Notice that the parameter count is the number of characters that are appended. The function `strncat()` appends, at most, the first `count` characters of `string2` to `string1`, terminates the resulting string with a null character, and then returns a pointer to the start of the concatenated string. If the value of parameter `count` exceeds the length of parameter `string2`, the function uses the length of that string instead of the value of parameter `count`. The argument for parameter `string1` should be able to store `count` + 1 characters.

The following is an example using the function `strncat()`:

```
char cString1[80] = "Hello ";
char cString2[80] = "World! How are you?";
strncat(cString1, cString2, strlen("World!"));
cout << cString1 << "\n"; // displays Hello World!
```

This example declares and initializes the two ASCIIZ string variables `cString1` and `cString2`. The example then uses the function `strncat()` to append a number of the characters [equal to the result of the expression `strlen("World!")`] in the string variable `cString2` to variable `cString1`. The output statement displays the characters `Hello World!`

Converting Strings

The STRING.H header file declares the functions `strupr()` and `strlwr()` to convert the characters of an ASCIIZ string into uppercase and lowercase, respectively.

Strupr function

The declaration of the function `strupr()` is as follows:

```
char *strupr(char *string);
```

The parameter `string` is the string to be capitalized. Notice that the function `strupr()` converts any lowercase letters in the string to uppercase and does not affect other characters. The function returns a pointer to the converted string.

The following is an example using the function `strupr()`:

```
char cString[10] = "oop";
strupr(cString);
cout << cString; // displays OOP
```

This example declares and initializes the ASCIIZ string variable `cString`. The example then converts the characters in that variable to uppercase by calling the function `strupr()` and passing that variable as the argument. Then the output statement displays the contents of the variable `cString`, which is the word `OOP`.

Strlwr function

The declaration of the function `strlwr()` is as follows:

```
char *strlwr(char *string);
```

The parameter `string` is the string to be converted into lower-case. Notice that the function `strlwr()` converts any uppercase letters into lowercase and does not affect other characters. The function returns a pointer to the converted string.

The following is an example using the function `strlwr`:

```
char cString[10] = "OOP";
strlwr(cString);
cout << cString; // displays oop
```

This example declares and initializes the ASCIIZ string variable `cString`. The example then converts the characters in that variable to lowercase by calling the function `strlwr()` and passing that variable as the argument. The output statement displays the contents of the variable `cString`, which is the word `oop`.

Copying Strings

The string library STRING.H declares the functions `strcpy()` and `strncpy()` to copy strings, because C++ does not enable you to copy ASCIIZ strings by using the operator =. Notice that the function `strcpy()` copies the entire characters of a source string. The function `strncpy()` copies a specified number of characters from the source string.

Strcpy function

The declaration of the function `strcpy()` is as follows:

```
char *strcpy(char *string1, const char *string2);
```

The parameter `string1` is the destination string, and the parameter `string2` is the source string. The function `strcpy()` copies `string2`, including the null terminator, to the location that is specified by `string1`; the function returns `string1`. Notice that the argument for parameter `string2` is expected to contain a null terminator. The function performs no overflow checking when copying or appending strings.

The following is an example using the function `strcpy()`:

```
char cStrSrc[80] = "Using a string function";
char cStrDest[80];
strcpy(cStrDest, cStrSrc);
cout << cStrDest << "\n";
```

This example declares the ASCIIZ string variables cStrSrc and cStrDest. The code initializes the first variable and uses the function strcpy() to copy the characters in variable cStrSrc to the variable cStrDest. The output statement displays the contents of the variable cStrDest (which stores the text Using a string function).

Strncpy function

The declaration for the function strncpy() is as follows:

```
char *strncpy(char *string1, const char *string2,
    size_t count);
```

The parameter string1 is the destination string, and the parameter string2 is the source string. Note that the parameter count represents the number of characters to copy. The function strncpy() copies count characters of string2 to string1 and then returns string1. If the argument of parameter count is less than the length of parameter string2, the function not does not automatically append a null terminator to the copied string. However, if the argument of parameter count is greater than the length of string2, the function pads string1 with null terminator characters up to the length count.

The following is an example of using the function strncpy():

```
char cStrSrc[80] = "Using a string function";
char cStrDest[10];
int nCount = 5;
strncpy(cStrDest, cStrSrc, nCount);
cout << cStrDest << "\n";
```

This example declares the ASCIIZ string variables cStrSrc and cStrDest and the int-type variable nCount. The code initializes the variables cStrSrc and nCount. Then the code uses the function strncpy() to copy the first nCount characters in variable cStrSrc to the variable cStrDest. The output statement displays the contents of the variable cStrDest (which is the text Using).

Finding Characters

The STRING.H header file declares the functions strchr() and strrchr(), which search for the first and last occurrence of a character in an ASCIIZ string, respectively.

Strchr function

The declaration of the function `strchr()` is as follows:

```
char *strchr(const char *string, int c);
```

The parameter `string` is the source string, and the parameter `c` is the search character. Notice that the function `strchr()` returns a pointer to the first occurrence of `c` (converted to a character) in the parameter `string`. If the converted character `c` is the null character, the function searches for the terminating null character in the parameter `string`. The function returns null if the character is not found.

The following is an example using the function `strchr()`:

```
char cString[81] = "The first time ever I saw your
    face";
char cSearch = 'h';
char* pStr = strchr(cString, cSearch);
int nOffset = pStr - cString;
// displays 'he first time ever I saw your face'
cout << pStr << endl;
cout << nOffset << endl; // displays 1
```

This example declares and initializes the string variable `cString` and the `char`-type variable `cSearch`. The code declares the string pointer `pStr` and initializes it with the result of calling function `strchr()`. Notice that the arguments for this function call are the variables `cString` and `cSearch`. The code also declares the `int`-type variable `nOffset` and initializes it with the expression `pStr - cString` (which is equal to 1). The first output statement displays the substring, accessed by the pointer `pStr`, `The first time ever I saw your face`. Then the second output statement displays the value of 1, which is stored in the variable `nOffset`.

Strrchr function

The function `strrchr()` searches for the last occurrence of a character in an ASCIIZ string. The declaration for the function `strrchr()` is as follows:

```
char *strrchr(const char *string, int c);
```

The parameter `string` is the searched string, and the parameter `c` is the search character. Notice that the `strrchr()` function locates the last occurrence of `c` (converted to `char`) in parameter `string`. The function returns a pointer to the last occurrence of the character in the searched string. If the function finds no match, it returns a null pointer.

The following is an example using the function `strrchr()`:

```
char cString[81] = "The first time ever I saw your
    face";
char cSearch = 'f';
char* pStr = strrchr(cString, cSearch);
int nOffset = pStr - cString;
// displays 'face'
cout << pStr << endl;
cout << nOffset << endl; // displays 31
```

This example declares and initializes the string variable `cString` and the `char`-type variable `cSearch`. Then the code declares the string pointer `pStr` and initializes it with the result of the calling function `strrchr()`. The arguments for this function call are the variables `cString` and `cSearch`. This code also declares the `int`-type variable `nOffset` and initializes it with the expression `pStr - cString` (which is equal to 31). The first output statement displays the substring, accessed by pointer `pStr`, `face`. Then the second output statement displays the value of 31, which is stored in the variable `nOffset`.

Strspn function

The function `strspn()` returns the index of the first character in a character set that is not in that set (an ASCIIZ string stores this set of characters). The declaration of the function `strspn()` is as follows:

```
size_t strspn(const char *string1, const char
    *string2);
```

The parameter `string1` is the searched string, and the parameter `string2` specifies the character set. Then the function `strspn()` returns the index of the first character in parameter `string1` that does not belong to the set of characters specified by the parameter `string2`. The function's result is equivalent to the length of the initial substring of parameter `string1`, which consists entirely of characters that are not in the parameter `string2`. The character search excludes the null terminator part of the parameter `string2`. If the parameter `string1` starts with a character that is not in parameter `string2`, the function `strspn()` yields 0.

The following is an example using the function `strspn()`:

```
char cString[81] = "355 / 113 = 3.14159";
char cCharSet[] = "1234567890+-*/=.";
int nIndex;
nIndex = strspn(cString, cCharSet);
cout << nIndex; // displays 3
```

This example declares and initializes the string variables cString and cCharSet. The variable cString is the searched variable, and the variable cCharSet stores the character set. This example also declares the int-type variable nIndex. The code searches for the first character in variable cString that is not in variable cCharSet by calling the function strspn(). This function returns 3, because the first occurrence of the space character (which is not in the character set) occurs at index 3. The output statement displays 3, the value in the variable nIndex.

Strcspn function

The function strcspn() returns the index of the first character in an ASCIIZ string that is part of a character set. The declaration of the function strcspn is as follows:

```
size_t strcspn(const char *string1, const char
    *string2);
```

The parameter string1 is the source string, and the parameter string2 specifies the character set. Notice that the function strcspn returns the index of the first character in parameter string1 belonging to the set of characters specified by the parameter string2. The function's result is equivalent to the length of the initial substring of parameter string1 that consists wholly of characters that are not in the parameter string2. This function does not include the null terminator in the search. If parameter string1 starts with a character from string2, the function strcspn() yields 0.

The following is an example using the function strcspn():

```
char cString[81] = "355 / 113 = 3.14159";
char cCharSet[] = "+-*/=.";
int nIndex;
nIndex = strcspn(cString, cCharSet);
cout << nIndex; // displays 4
```

This example declares and initializes the string variables cString and cCharSet. The variable cString is the searched variable, and the variable cCharSet stores the character set. The example also declares the int-type variable nIndex. This code searches for the first character in variable cString that is in variable cCharSet by calling the function strcspn(). This function returns 4, because the first occurrence of the slash (/) character (which is in the character set) occurs at index 4. The output statement displays 4, the value in the variable nIndex.

Finding Substrings

The STRING.H header file declares the function `strstr`, which searches for an ASCIIZ substring in an ASCIIZ string. The declaration of the function `strstr` is as follows:

```
char *strstr(const char *string1, const char
    *string2);
```

The parameter `string1` is the searched string, and the parameter `string2` is the search string. Notice that the function `strstr` returns a pointer to the first occurrence of parameter `string2` in parameter `string1`. If the search fails, the function yields a null pointer.

The following is an example using the function `strstr`:

```
char cString[81] = "355 / 113 = 3.14159";
char cSearch[] = "113";
char *pStr;
pStr = strstr(cString, cSearch);
cout << pStr; // displays 113 = 3.14159
```

This example declares and initializes the string variables `cString` and `cSearch`. The variable `cString` is the searched variable, and the variable `cSearch` stores the search string. Notice that the example also declares the `int`-type variable `nIndex`. This code searches for the first occurrence of the substring 113 in variable `cString` by calling the function `strstr`. The function returns a pointer to the substring 113 = 3.14159 and assigns it to the pointer `pStr`. Then the output statement displays the string 113 = 3.14159.

Getting the Length of a String

The STRING.H header file declares the function `strlen()`, which returns the number of characters in an ASCIIZ string. The declaration of the function `strlen()` is as follows:

```
size_t strlen(const char *string);
```

The parameter `string` is the ASCIIZ string. Notice that the function returns the length, in bytes, of the argument for the parameter `string`. This function result excludes the null terminator. The type `size_t` is compatible with various predefined integer types.

The following is an example using the function `strlen()`:

```
char cName[30];
do {
  cout << "Enter your name : ";
  cin.getline(cName, sizeof(cName) - 1);
} while (strlen(cName) == 0);
cout << "Hello " << cName << ". How are you!";
```

This example declares the string variable `cName` and uses a `do-while` loop to prompt you for your name. Then the loop iterates until you enter a name. The `while` clause uses the function `strlen()` to examine the length of the string in the variable `cName`.

Initializing Strings

C++ enables you to declare an ASCIIZ string (as an array of characters) and initialize it with a string literal. The general syntax for declaring and initializing an ASCIIZ string is as follows:

```
char stringName[numberOfCharacters] = "text";
```

The following are examples of declaring and initializing ASCIIZ strings:

```
char cGreeting[30] = "Hello World!";
char cMessage[] = "Your machine will explode in
    100_ years!";
```

This code declares and initializes the string variable `cGreetings`. The variable has 30 characters (including the null character) and stores the initializing string literal `"Hello World!"` Then the second example declares the ASCIIZ string variable `cMessage` without explicitly specifying the number of characters. The compiler sets the number of characters equal to the number of characters in the initializing string plus one. (The extra character stores the null terminator.)

Reversing Strings

The STRING.H header file declares the function `strrev()`, which reverses the characters in an ASCIIZ string. The declaration of the function `strrev()` is as follows:

```
char *strrev(char *string);
```

The parameter `string` is the string whose characters are reversed by the function. Notice that the function does not alter the location of the null terminator. The function returns a pointer to the altered string.

The following is an example using the function `strrev()`:

```
char cString[10] = "Did";
strrev(cString);
cout << cString; // displays diD
```

This example declares and initializes the ASCIIZ string variable
cString. The example then reverses the characters in that
variable by calling the function strrev() and passing that
variable as the argument. Then the output statement displays the
contents of the variable cString, which is diD.

Part XII

Classes

Classes bring object-oriented programming to C++. Classes promote a new way of thinking and programming, because they encourage you to represent objects as animated things that have attributes and operations. For example, you can use a class to represent a simple four-function calculator. The calculator class could contain parts that store the numbers you key into the calculator. This class could also include functions that support the calculator's arithmetic operations.

This part covers various aspects of declaring classes, class hierarchies, and the components of classes. Not only do I discuss the big picture relating to classes, but I also talk about the nuts and bolts that make up a class.

In this part . . .

- ✔ Constructors
- ✔ Declaring data members
- ✔ Declaring classes
- ✔ Declaring class instances
- ✔ Destructors
- ✔ Exceptions
- ✔ Friend functions
- ✔ Member Functions
- ✔ Nested data types
- ✔ Operators
- ✔ Static members

Constructors

Constructors are special members that initialize class instances. The compiler generates code that automatically invokes an appropriate constructor when you create a class instance. The general syntax for declaring a constructor in a class is as follows:

```
class className
{
public:
// void constructor
className();
// copy constructor
className(className& classNameObject);
// additional constructor
className(parameterList);
// other members

};
```

C++ has the following rules about declaring and using constructors:

✦ The name of the constructor must match the name of its class.

✦ A constructor may have a parameter list to help fine-tune the creation of class instances.

✦ A class may have multiple constructors to enable its instances to be initialized differently.

✦ A constructor with no parameters (or with a parameter list that has default arguments for each parameter) is called the *void* or *default* constructor.

✦ A constructor with one parameter that has the class type is called the *copy* constructor.

✦ The declaration of an array of instances requires the use of the default constructor.

✦ If the class does not declare a constructor, C++ creates a default constructor for that class.

✦ C++ invokes a constructor when you create a class instance. The arguments of that instance select the appropriate constructor if the class declares multiple constructors.

If you make all the constructors of a class either protected or private, you cannot create instances of that class. This kind of class serves more as a parent to child classes.

The following is an example of a class that uses multiple constructors to support different ways to initialize class instances. This example contains a new version of the class `myPoint`. The version contains three constructors: the default constructor, the copy constructor, and an additional constructor.

```
#include <iostream.h>
#include <math.h>

inline double sqr(double x)
{ return x * x; }

class myPoint
{
 public:
 myPoint();
 myPoint(const myPoint& otherPoint)
 { copyCoords(otherPoint); }
 myPoint(double fX, double fY);

 // other members

 protected:
 double m_fX;
 double m_fY;
};

myPoint::myPoint()
{
 m_fX = 0.;
 m_fY = 0.;
}

myPoint::myPoint(double fX, double fY)
{
 m_fX = fX;
 m_fY = fY;
}

void myPoint::copyCoords(const myPoint& otherPoint)
{
 m_fX = otherPoint.m_fX;
 m_fY = otherPoint.m_fY;
}
```

The highlights of the preceding source code are the three constructors of class `myPoint`:

✦ The default constructor assigns zeros to the data members `m_fX` and `m_fY`.

✦ The copy constructor copies the values in the data members of parameter `otherPoint` to their counterparts in the initialized instance.

◆ The constructor myPoint(double, double) initializes the data members m_fX and m_fY by using the arguments of parameters fX and fY, respectively.

Declaring Classes — the Basics

C++ enables you to declare a class that represents some object that you want to work with in your program. The following is the general syntax for declaring a class:

```
class className
{
  [public:]
public data members
public member functions
  [protected:]
protected data members
protected member functions
  [private:]
private data members
private member functions
};
```

The declaration of a class contains the following parts:

◆ The keyword class, which tells the compiler that you are declaring a class.

◆ The name of the class, which you select.

◆ The opening brace, which starts the class declaration.

◆ The optional keyword public:, which starts declaring the public data members and/or member functions. The public members of a class are highly accessible by other program parts. I discuss more about public members later in this part.

◆ The optional keyword protected:, which starts declaring the protected data members and/or member functions. The protected members of a class are moderately accessible by other program parts. I discuss more about protected members later in this part.

◆ The optional keyword private:, which starts declaring the private data members and/or member functions. The private members of a class are minimally accessible by other program parts. I discuss more about private members later in this part.

◆ The closing brace followed by a semicolon, which ends the declaration of the class.

C++ requires you to observe the following rules about the public, protected, and private sections of a class:

◆ The public, protected, and private sections are optional. If you don't specify a section type by name, the compiler assumes that the section is private. In other words, private is the default setting.

◆ The public, protected, and private sections can occur in any order.

◆ The class declaration may contain multiple combinations of public, protected, and private sections.

◆ The public, protected, and private sections may be empty when they don't declare data members or member functions.

Each section can declare data members and/or member functions (collectively called *members*). The data member looks like the declaration of a variable except that data members can't have an initial value. The general syntax for declaring a data member is as follows:

```
dataType dataMemberName;
```

Here, the general syntax indicates that you can't initialize a data member in a class declaration. The following are examples of data members that support a moving object:

```
double fXCoord;
double fYCoord;
```

This example declares the double-type data members fXCoord and fYCoord, which represent the *X* and *Y* coordinates of an object, respectively. Some programmers advocate starting the name of a data member with the characters m_ (for *member*) to improve the readability of the source code. When you see a name that starts with m_, you know that it refers to a data member. Applying the preceding style to the preceding examples yields the following:

```
double m_fXCoord;
double m_fYCoord;
```

Member functions are the methods that support the operations of the class. Declaring a member function looks like declaring a function prototype. The general syntax for declaring a member function is as follows:

```
returnType functionName([optionalParameterList]);
```

Examples of member functions are as follows:

```
void moveTo(double fnewXCoord, double fnewYCoord);
void moveBy(double fXchange, double fYchange);
double getXCoord();
double getYCoord();
```

The first example declares the member function moveTo(), which has a void return type and the double-type parameters fnewXCoord and fnewYCoord. The member function simulates moving the object to a new location specified by the argument that is supplied to the parameters newXCoord and newYCoord. (That's a simplified explanation.)

The second member function is moveBy(), which has a void return type and the double-type parameters fXchange and fYchange. Notice that the member function simulates moving an object by specifying the vertical and horizontal distances traveled. The parameters fXchange and fYchange specify these distances, respectively.

The last two member functions, getXCoord() and getYCoord(), have the return type double and are without parameters. The member function getXCoord(), as the name suggests, returns the X coordinates. Likewise, the member function getYCoord() returns the Y coordinates.

The earlier examples in this section show you the components of a class, piece by piece. Putting the preceding parts together in a class declaration yields the following source code, which shows a complete declaration of a class. The following is the source code for the class Rabbit, which represents an electronic rabbit that you can move over a plain surface by specifying a new location to go to or by specifying a move relative to the current location. You can also inquire about the location of the rabbit. The following is the class declaration:

```
class Rabbit
{
    public:
    // move object to a new location
    void moveTo(double fnewXCoord, double fnewYCoord);
    // move object by displacing it
    void moveBy(double fXchange, double fYchange);
    // obtain the X coordinate
    double getXCoord();
    // obtain the Y coordinate
    double getYCoord();
```

```
protected:
double m_fXCoord;  // X coordinate
double m_fYCoord;  // Y coordinate
};
```

The preceding code declares the class Rabbit, which has the public and protected sections (more about these sections later in this part). The public section declares the member functions moveTo( ), moveBy( ), getXCoord( ), and getYCoord( ). The class declares a protected section that contains the declaration of the double-type data members m_fXCoord and m_fYCoord.

Public section

C++ enables you to declare a class with public, protected, and private sections. Each section supports a specific level of accessibility to the class members. Therefore, C++ classes support three levels of access by the class instances and by classes that are descendants of that class. What about access by other member functions in the same class? C++ supports a simple rule: All member functions have access to all other data members and member functions in the same class, regardless of what sections these members are declared in. In addition, functions that aren't part of any class, such as function main( ), and classes that aren't related at all to current class can also access public members of a class.

The *public section* tells the compiler that the data members and member functions in that section are accessible to everything: *All* functions in the program [such as the function main( )] can access public methods and data whether they are instances of the class, descendants, or neither.

Programming gurus recommend that the data members not be declared in the public section. Why? Public access to data members makes them vulnerable to unwanted manipulation (or access) by class instances (that is, objects that belong to that class) as well as regular functions that don't belong to the class. Such manipulation can very well lead to *logically* corrupting the data in the data members. In other words, free access to data members allows a program to store bad data that is valid as far as the runtime system goes but makes no sense in the logic of the program.

Protected section

The *protected section* contains data members and member functions that are not accessible to the class instances and functions that do not belong to the class [such as the function main()]. Typically, the protected section contains data members and *auxiliary* member functions (that is, member functions that work behind the scene to help other member functions, especially the ones declared in the public section).

The following is an example that declares the class dataBroker:

```
class dataBroker
{
 public:
    int Search(int nSearchVal)
    // other data members and member functions
    // declared here

 protected:
    bool m_bDataIsSorted;
    // other data members declared here

    int BinarySearch(int nSearchVal);
    int LinearSearch(int nSearchVal);
    // other member functions declared here
};
```

The class dataBroker has the following components:

+ The public member function Search()

+ The data member m_bDataIsSorted, which keeps track of whether the data is sorted

+ The protected member function BinarySearch(), which conducts an efficient search if the data is sorted

+ The protected member function LinearSearch(), which conducts an inefficient search if the data is not sorted

The public member function Search() invokes either protected member function BinarySearch() or LinearSearch(), depending on the Boolean value of the data member m_bDataIsSorted. Therefore, the protected member functions are *auxiliary,* because they serve the public member function Search().

Private section

The *private section* contains data members and member functions that are not accessible to the class instances, to descendant classes, or to functions that do not belong to the class [such as the function `main()`]. Typically, the private section contains highly sensitive data members and auxiliary member functions. By *highly sensitive,* I mean those data members that should work only with the private member functions of the class. In other words, private data members are conceptually "top secret" and should be handled by member functions that are themselves private. How do these private member functions work with the rest of the class members? You can have public and protected member functions access the private member functions (but not the private data members). In the case of a single class, the protected and private sections seem to have the same effect. When are private and protected sections different? The answer lies in creating descendant classes.

The next sample code shows an example of how private sections work, using the class `superDataBroker`:

```
class superDataBroker
{
  public:
      int Search(int nSearchVal)
      // other data members and member functions
      // declared here

  protected:
      bool m_bDataIsSorted;
      // other data members declared here

      int BinarySearch(int nSearchVal);
      int LinearSearch(int nSearchVal);
      // other member functions declared here

  private:
      int m_nSearchDataBuffer;
};
```

The declaration of class `superDataBroker` is similar to that of class `dataBroker`, except that the `superDataBroker` class has the private `int`-type data member `m_nSearchDataBuffer`. This data member stores part of the database to speed the search.

Also, assume that the class uses a special method to search data (involving the data member `m_nSearchDataBuffer`). Therefore, by declaring data member `m_nSearchDataBuffer`, you prevent other descendant classes from accessing this member and altering the search scheme. Why? To ensure that the data member works exclusively with the special search method in the class `superDataBroker`. This way, no descendant class can alter the search method and perhaps make it less efficient or introduce errors.

Declaring Objects (Or Class Instances)

When you declare a class, you declare a new data type that represents a category of objects. As with predefined data types, you can declare variables whose type is the class that you just defined. These special variables are examples of the objects that you represent with your own class.

Programmers use special terms for these kinds of variables: *class instances* or *objects*. Therefore, a class instance (or object) is an example, so to speak, of the class you defined. The declaration of a class instance has the following general syntax:

className classInstance;

Consider the following example:

```
Rabbit BugsBunny;
Rabbit EasterBunny;
```

This code declares two instances of class `Rabbit`: `BugsBunny` and `EasterBunny`. Each instance has its own versions of data members `m_fXCoord` and `m_fYCoord`. The runtime system invokes the void constructor for each instance and assigns zeros in the data members `m_fXCoord` and `m_fYCoord` of each instance.

You should think of class instances as objects, not as variables (although, technically, class instances *are* special kinds of variables). The notion of an *object* is that it represents an entity that can receive a message from you and then respond to the message by invoking a member function. The term *sending a message to an object* is part of object-oriented thinking. This thinking promotes the paradigm of communicating with objects by sending them messages. In fact, the big picture in object-oriented program has the various parts of a program (which are objects) communicate with each other. Like function calls, messages often have arguments. Moreover, I use the term C++ message in this book to make a distinction from Windows (3.*x*, 95, and NT) messages that are sent to windows, dialog boxes, visual controls, and so on.

The following is a fully implemented class that is based on the class `Rabbit`, which I present in the preceding section "Declaring Classes — the Basics." This implementation uses random numbers to change to coordinates of the object `Bunny`, the instance of the class `Rabbit`. The following is a sample session with the complete program that requires no input from you:

```
Bunny at (31, 31)
Bunny at (40.1, 40.1)
Bunny at (18, 18)
```

```
Bunny at (19.6, 19.6)
Bunny at (27, 27)
Bunny at (32.9, 32.9)
Bunny at (80, 80)
Bunny at (86.1, 86.1)
Bunny at (22, 22)
Bunny at (26.8, 26.8)
```

The following is the source code for the program that declares the class `Rabbit` and uses its instances.

```cpp
#include <iostream.h>
#include <stdlib.h>

const int MAX_COORD = 100;

// declare function prototype
double getNewCoord();
double getShiftInCoord();

// declare class
class Rabbit
{
   public:
       // declare the constructor
       Rabbit();
       // move object to a new location
     void moveTo(double fnewXCoord, double
     fnewYCoord);
       // move object by displacing it
       void moveBy(double fXchange, double fYchange);
       // obtain the X coordinate
       double getXCoord()
       { return m_fXCoord; }
       // obtain the Y coordinate
       double getYCoord()
       { return m_fYCoord; }

   protected:
       double m_fXCoord; // X coordinate
       double m_fYCoord; // Y coordinate
};

Rabbit::Rabbit()
{
   m_fXCoord = 0;
   m_fYCoord = 0;
}

void Rabbit::moveTo(double fnewXCoord, double
   fnewYCoord)
{
   m_fXCoord = fnewXCoord;
   m_fYCoord = fnewYCoord;
}
```

(continued)

(continued)

```
void Rabbit::moveBy(double fXchange, double
    fYchange)
{
    m_fXCoord = m_fXCoord + fXchange;
    m_fYCoord = m_fYCoord + fYchange;
}

main()
{
    const int MAX_MOVES = 10;
    Rabbit Bunny;
    for(int i = 0; i < MAX_MOVES; i += 2) {
        // use moveTo member function
        Bunny.moveTo(getNewCoord(), getNewCoord());
        cout << "Bunny at (" << Bunny.getXCoord()
             << ", " << Bunny.getXCoord() << ")\n";
        // use moveBy member function
        Bunny.moveBy(getShiftInCoord(),
        getShiftInCoord());
        cout << "Bunny at (" << Bunny.getXCoord()
             << ", " << Bunny.getXCoord() << ")\n";
    }

    return 0;
}

double getNewCoord()
{
    return (rand() % MAX_COORD + 1);
}

double getShiftInCoord()
{
    return (rand() % MAX_COORD + 1) / 10.0;
}
```

The declaration and implementation of class `Rabbit` should be familiar to you by now, so I can focus on the other parts of the source code. The code declares the constant `MAX_COORD` to specify the maximum values for the *X* and *Y* coordinates. This code also declares the prototypes for the functions `getNewCoord()` and `getShiftInCoord()`.

The function `getNewCoord()` returns a random coordinate value for either the *X* or *Y* coordinate. This function uses the function `rand()`, which is declared in the header file STDLIB.H.

The function `getShiftInCoord()` returns a random shift in the coordinate value for either the *X* or *Y* coordinate. This function also uses the function `rand()`.

The source code defines the function main( ), which declares the following local items:

✦ The constant MAX_MOVES, which specifies the number of moves for the instance of the class Rabbit

✦ The object Bunny, which is an instance of the class Rabbit

The function main( ) uses a for loop (which is a special program part that executes other statements many times) to perform the following tasks:

✦ Moves the object Bunny to a new set of random coordinates. This task involves sending the C++ message moveTo( ) to the object Bunny. The arguments for this message are two calls to function getNewCoord( ). This task involves invoking the member function Rabbit::moveTo.

✦ Displays the current coordinates of the object Bunny. This task involves sending the C++ messages getXCoord( ) and getYCoord( ) to the object Bunny to obtain the *X* and *Y* coordinates, respectively, invoking the member functions Rabbit::getXCoord and Rabbit::GetYCoord( ).

✦ Shifts the object Bunny to a new set of random coordinates. This task involves sending the C++ message moveBy( ) to the object Bunny. The arguments for this message are two calls to the function getShiftInCoord( ). The task involves invoking the member function Rabbit::moveBy.

✦ Displays the current coordinates of the object Bunny. This task involves sending the C++ messages getXCoord( ) and getYCoord( ) to the object Bunny to obtain the *X* and *Y* coordinates, respectively, and invoking the member functions Rabbit::getXCoord and Rabbit::GetYCoord( ).

Destructors

Destructors are special members that uninitialize class instances when they reach the end of their scope. The general syntax for declaring a destructor in a class is as follows:

```
class className
{
public:
// void constructor
className();
// other constructors
// destructor
~className();
other members
};
```

C++ has the following rules about declaring and using destructors:

✦ The name of the destructor must match the name of its class and must start with the tilde character (~).

✦ A destructor has no parameter list.

✦ A class has only one destructor.

✦ If the class does not declare a destructor, C++ creates a default destructor for that class.

✦ C++ automatically invokes the destructor of a class instance when that instance reaches the end if its scope.

You need to declare a destructor to perform cleanup operations for the class instances. The following are examples of cleanup operations:

✦ The class uses a constructor to create dynamic data. The destructor removes the memory space that was occupied by that data.

✦ The class constructor opens a file for input or output. The destructor closes that file.

✦ The destructor displays text enabling you to trace the removal of class instances.

The following is a simple example of a class that uses a constructor and destructor to manage dynamic arrays:

```cpp
#include <iostream.h>
#include <string.h>

class myArray
{
 public:
 myArray(int nNumElems = 10);
 ~myObject();
 // other member functions

 protected:
 int* m_pData;
 int m_nNumData;
};

myArray::myArray(int nNumElems)
{
 m_nNumData = nNumElems;
 m_pData = new int[nNumElems];
}

myArray::~myArray()
{
 delete [] m_pData;
}
```

This example shows you the class myArray, which creates a dynamic array that is accessed by the data member m_pData. The constructor allocates the dynamic space of the array. The destructor removes the dynamic array that is accessed by the data member m_pData using the operator delete.

Exceptions

C++ supports exceptions and exception handing to detect and manage runtime error. The word *exception* comes from the *exceptional program flow* that occurs during a runtime error.

C++ makes use of classes and objects in handling exceptions. C++ uses the terms *throwing* and *catching* to describe handling exceptions. Either the runtime or your code throws exceptions. To handle the thrown exceptions, you need to catch these exceptions and handle them.

Exception classes

C++ makes use of classes to represent and encapsulate exceptions. There arc two general kinds of classes that model exceptions:

+ *Skeleton classes.* These classes have no members, because their names are sufficient to refer to and handle the exception.

+ *Classes with data members.* These classes declare data members that allow them to better describe the exception.

The following are examples of exception classes:

```
class badInputException {};
class badRangeException {};
class badFileException
{
  public:
    char m_pszFilename[31];
};
```

The first two examples are skeleton classes that model exceptions handling input and a range of values. These classes have no members. The last example declares an exception class that has the data member m_pszFilename. This class supposedly uses this data member to describe which file failed I/O operations.

Standard exceptions

C++ defines a set of basic exception classes that represent the most common runtime errors. The following table lists these exceptions and indicates their lineage.

Exception Class	Parent Class	Purpose
exception	None	The base class for all of the exceptions thrown by the C++ standard library
logic_error	Exception	Reports logical program errors that can detected *before* the program proceeds to execute subsequent statements
runtime_error	Exception	Reports runtime errors that are detected *when* the program executes certain statements
ios::failure	Exception	Reports stream I/O errors
domain_error	logic_error	Reports infraction of a condition
invalid_argument	logic_error	Signals that the argument of a function is not valid
length_error	logic_error	Signals that an operation attempts to create an object with a length that exceeds or is equal to NPOS (the largest value of the type size_t)
out_of_range	logic_error	Signals that an argument is out of range
bad_cast	logic_error	Reports an invalid dynamic cast expression during runtime identification
bad_typeid	logic_error	Reports a null pointer in a type identifying expression
range_error	runtime_error	Signals invalid postcondition
overflow_error	runtime_error	Signals arithmetic overflow
bad_alloc	runtime_error	Signals the failure of dynamic allocation

Throwing an exception

C++ offers the throw statement to throw an exception (which is a predefined data item or an instance of an exception class). The general syntax for the throw statement is as follows:

```
throw exceptionObject;
```

The exceptionObject can a predefined type or an exception class instance. The latter can be a previously declared instance or a temporary instance that was created by using the constructor of the exception class.

The following are examples of throwing exceptions:

```
class badValueException
{
  public:
    badValueException(int nVal = 0)
      { cout << nVal << " is a bad value\n"; }
};

int nBadVal;

throw badValueException(100);
throw nBadVal;
```

This code shows two `throw` statements. The first one throws an instance of an exception class, and the second throws an `int`-type variable. Notice that I have not yet introduced the `try` statement, which should contain the `throw` statements. Also, I have not introduced the `catch` statement, which catches the exceptions.

Try block

Throwing an exception occurs in a `try` block. This causes the compiler to pay special attention to generating code for handling exceptions. The general syntax for the `try` block is as follows:

```
try {
  statements that may throw one or more exceptions
}
```

The `try` block contains any statement that may raise an exception, including `throw` statements. The following is an example of a `try` block:

```
class badValueException
{
  public:
    badValueException(int nVal = 0)
      { cout << nVal << " is a bad value\n"; }
};

main()
{
  int nBadVal;

  try {
    throw badValueException(100);
  }
  // statements to handle the exception
  return 0;
}
```

This code shows a `try` block that contains a `throw` statement. The statements that follow the `try` block handle the exceptions that are raised in the `try` block. The following section discusses the exception-handling `catch` handler.

Catch clauses

C++ offers the `catch` clauses (or handlers) to work with the `try` block. The `catch` handlers have a logic that is similar to that of the `case` clauses of a `switch` statement. The general syntax for a `catch` handler is as follows:

```
catch(exceptionType [exceptionObject]) {
  // statements that handle or rethrow the
    exception
}
```

A `catch` clause declares an exception type and an optional exception parameter. You need this parameter if it passes additional information that is related to the exception. You can use multiple catch handlers as well as the special `catch(...)` clause to catch and handle exceptions, as shown in the following general syntax:

```
catch(exceptionType1 [exceptionObject1]) {
  // statements that handle or rethrow
    exceptionType1
}
catch(exceptionType2 [exceptionObject2]) {
  // statements that handle or rethrow the
    exceptionType2
}
catch(exceptionType3 [exceptionObject3]) {
  // statements that handle or rethrow the
    exceptionType3
}
catch(...) {
  // statements that handle or rethrow the all
    other exceptions
}
```

Unlike the `else` or default clauses of an `if` or `switch` statement, use the `catch(...)` handler carefully, because it can trap errors that you did not anticipate.

The following is an example of using the `try` block with the `catch` clauses:

```
class myError1 {};
class myError2
{
  public:
   myError2(int nError)
```

```
        { m_nError = nError; }
      int m_nError;
};

main()
{
  int nVal = -1;

  try {
    throw myError2(nVal);
  }
  catch(int nError) {
    cout << "Handling int exception\n";
    cout << nError << " is invalid\n";
  }
  catch(myError1) {
    cout << "Handling myError1 exception\n";
  }
  catch(myError2 errObj) {
    cout << "Handling myError2 exception\n";
    cout << errObj.m_nError << " is invalid\n";
  }
  catch(...) {
    cout << "Handling other errors\n";
  }

  return 0;
}
```

This example declares the exception classes myError1 and
myError2. The first exception class is a skeleton class, whereas
the second class has the public data member m_nError. The class
myError2 has a constructor that initializes the data member
m_nError. Then the function main() declares and initializes the
int-type variable nVal. The function has a try block that contains a throw statement, which throws a myError2 exception (by
using the value in the variable nVal). The function main has the
following catch clauses:

+ The catch(int nError) clause, which catches exceptions
  that have the int type. This clause displays a message and
  the value of the parameter nError.

+ The catch(myError1) clause, which catches myError1
  exceptions. This clause has no parameter and simply displays
  a message.

+ The catch(myError2 errObj) clause, which catches
  myError2 exceptions. This clause displays a message and
  then displays the data member errObj.m_nError. The
  clause shows you how to use the exception parameter.

+ The catch(...) clause, which catches all other exceptions.

Friend Functions

Friend functions are special nonmember functions that you declare
in a class. A friend function has the same access privilege of a
member function. Friend functions may violate the true spirit of
object-oriented programming to offer you convenient coding! A
friend function is a regular function that you call (that is, it is not a
member function) such that one of its arguments must be an
instance of the host class (or the befriended class, if you prefer).
Thus the friend function can declare the first parameter to have a
type that is not of the befriended class.

The general syntax for declaring a friend function in a class is as
follows:

```
class className
{
 // declaration of members
 friend returnType functionName(parameterList);
};
```

Notice that you declare a friend function by placing the keyword
friend before the function's return type. The definition of a friend
function does not require using the keyword friend. The parameter list of a friend function may have any number and type of
parameters as long as one parameter has the type of the befriended class.

The following is an example of a class declaring friend functions:

```
class myComplex
{
 public:
 myComplex();
 // declaration of other members

 friend myComplex DivideComplex(myComplex& C,
    double fReal);
 friend myComplex DivideComplex(double fReal,
    myComplex& C);

 // declaration of other members
};
```

This example shows the class myComplex with the overloaded
friend function DivideComplex(). The first version of this
function has the myComplex&-type parameter C and the double-
type parameter fReal. Then the second version of the function
declares these parameters in reverse sequence. The friend
function DivideComplex() returns the type myComplex. Notice

that the second version of function `DivideComplex` has a
`double`-type parameter as the first parameter and not a
`myComplex&`-type parameter.

Member Functions

A class typically declares data members and member functions.
Descriptions are as follows:

✦ The *data members* store information that describes the
attributes of the objects that are being represented by the
class.

✦ The *member functions* specify the operations that access and
manipulate the values in the data members.

Data members of a class enable the class to represent the various
attributes of the objects that it supports. Remember, a class can
declare data members that have predefined types, user-defined
types, or even other classes.

The member functions of a class support the operations of that
class. These functions may supply the class instances with new
data, query existing information in the class instances, or perform
operations based on the information that is stored in the data
members. For example, if you define a class to represent an
electronic version of a CD player (the kind that you may see in
Windows or Windows 95), you have data members that store the
sound volume, musical track currently being played, and so forth.
The CD player class would have a member function that sets and
queries the sound volume by accessing the data member that
stores the player's sound volume. Likewise, the class would have
member functions that select the next musical track, select the
last music track, or select a track at random. Each of these
member functions would access the data member that stores the
track number to determine the current musical track number.

The source code needs to *define* (that is, implement) the member
functions of a class. Typically, you define a member function after
the class declaration. The location of the member function
definition can be in the same file with the class declaration or in a
separate file. This inclusion is necessary for the compiler to see
the class declaration first. In simple programs, such as the ones in
this book, you can place the declarations and definitions in the
same file (a CPP file). In more complex programs, you separate the
declarations and definitions in separate files. To use separate files,
you place the class declaration in an H header file and the definitions of the member functions in a CPP file, which must include
the H header file.

Use the following general syntax to define a C++ member function:

```
returnType
    className::functionName([optionalParameterlist])
{
    // statements that define the member function
    [return returnedValue;]
}
```

The preceding syntax shows the following parts that are used to define a member function:

✦ The return type, which shows the data type of the result that is returned by the member function.

✦ The name of the class that owns the member function. This is the name of the class to which the member function belongs.

✦ The scope resolution operator (two colon characters).

✦ The name of the member function that you select.

✦ The optional parameter list. This list must match the parameter list in the class declaration.

✦ The opening brace, which begins the member function body.

✦ The function's code: the statements that implement what the member function does.

✦ The return statements, which yield the function's result for non-void member functions only.

✦ The closing brace, which ends the member function body.

The following is an example of a class declaration followed by the implementation of its member functions:

```
class Rabbit
{
  public:
    // move object to a new location
    void moveTo(double fnewXCoord, double
fnewYCoord);
    // move object by displacing it
    void moveBy(double fXchange, double fYchange);
    // obtain the X coordinate
    double getXCoord();
    // obtain the Y coordinate
    double getYCoord();

  protected:
    double m_fXCoord; // X coordinate
    double m_fYCoord; // Y coordinate
};
```

```
void Rabbit::moveTo(double fnewXCoord, double
   fnewYCoord)
{
   m_fXCoord = fnewXCoord;
   m_fYCoord = fnewYCoord;
}

void Rabbit::moveBy(double fXchange, double
   fYchange);
{
   m_fXCoord = m_fXCoord + fXchange;
   m_fYCoord = m_fYCoord + fYchange;
}

double Rabbit::getXCoord()
{
   return m_fXCoord;
}

double Rabbit::getYCoord()
{
   return m_fYCoord;
}
```

This code shows the definition of the member functions
moveTo(), moveBy(), getXCoord(), and getYCoord(). The
statements in these member functions set and query the values in
the data members m_fXCoord and m_fYCoord. Notice that the
first two member functions assign new values to the data members
by using the parameters of the member functions.

The following statements further describe the code:

✦ The member function moveTo() assigns the arguments of
   parameters fnewXCoord and fnewYCoord to the data
   members m_fXCoord and m_fYCoord, respectively.

✦ The member function moveBy() increases the values of the
   data members m_fXCoord and m_fYCoord by the arguments
   of the parameters fXchange and fYchange, respectively.

✦ The member function getXCoord() returns the value in the
   data member m_fXCoord.

✦ The member function getYCoord() returns the value in the
   data member m_fYCoord.

C++ enables you to place the declaration and implementation in
separate files, especially when you write a library of classes. This
is because you provide the H header files for the class library and
provide a compiled form (not the source code) of the CPP files to
other programmers. Thus the class library (that is, a class defined

in a library of classes) cannot change the implementation source code when you give other programmers the compiled form only — but they can still use the class library in their programs.

Nested Data Types

C++ enables you to declare enumerated types, structures, and classes that are nested inside other classes. These nested types provide special support to the host class. By declaring the nested types in the public sections, you can make them available to other classes and functions. In this case, the names of the nested types and their members must be qualified with the name of the host class. The following sections discuss nested classes in more detail and show you examples of using them.

Nested classes

C++ enables you to declare a class that is nested inside another class. The nested class mainly serves to support the host class. If you declare the nested class as public, you can use it in nonmember functions. In this case, you must qualify the name of the nested class with the name of the host class.

The following is an example of a class that declares a nested class:

```
class FindLostPersonGame
{
  public:
    FindLostPersonGame(int nMaxAttempts = 100);
    void Play();

  protected:
    // nested class
    class Point
    {
      public:
        Point();
        Point(int nX, int nY);
        Point(Point& aLoc);
        void MoveTo(Point newLoc);
        double GetDistance(Point& aNotherPoint);
        int m_nX;
        int m_nY;
    };

    Point m_LostPersonLoc;  // location of lost
person
    Point m_YourLoc; // location of rescuer
    int m_nNumAttempts;
    int m_nMaxAttempts;
```

```
      bool isFound();
      void initGame();
      void AskForNewLoc();
};
```

This example declares the class FindLostPersonGame, which
simulates rescuing a lost person. The class declares a public
constructor and the public member function Play(). Notice that
the class declares the following items in the protected section:

+ The nested class Point. This class has a default constructor,
  a custom constructor, a copy constructor, the member
  function MoveTo(), the member function GetDistance(),
  and the int-type members m_nX and m_nY (which store the
  location). This class manages a location.

+ The Point-type data member m_LostPersonLoc, which
  stores the location of the lost person.

+ The Point-type data member m_YourLoc, which stores the
  location of the rescuing person.

+ The int-type data member m_nNumAttempts, which stores
  the number of rescue attempts.

+ The int-type data member m_nMaxAttempts, which stores
  the maximum number of rescue attempts.

+ The bool-type member function isFound(). This member
  returns true if you found the lost person.

+ The member function initGame(), which initializes the
  game.

+ The member function AskForNewLoc(), which prompts you
  for a new search location. This member returns a Point-type
  result.

The previous example shows that a class can use a nested class to
declare data members. The member functions of the nested class
support the operations of this kind of data members (which are
instances of nested classes).

Nested enumerated types

C++ enables you to declare nested enumerated types in a class.
The nested enumerated type mainly serves its host class. If you
declare the enumerated type as nonpublic, you cannot use it in
nonmember functions (either as parameters or as local variables).
By contrast, if you declare the enumerated type as public, you can
use it in nonmember functions.

The following is an example that illustrates nested enumerated types:

```cpp
class Days
{
 public:
   enum Logical { FALSE, TRUE };

 protected:
   enum weekDays { Sunday = 1, Monday, Tuesday,
   Wednesday, Thursday, Friday, Saturday };

   weekDays m_eDay;
   char m_pszDay[10];

 public:
   Days(const char* pszDay = "Sunday")
   { assignDay(pszDay); }

   Logical assignDay(const char* pszDay =
   "Sunday");
   char* getDay();
   void nextDay();
   void prevDay();
   void addDays(unsigned uMoreDays);
};

Days::Logical Days::assignDay(const char* pszDay)
{
 Logical ok = TRUE;

 if (strcmpi(pszDay, "Sunday") == 0)
   m_eDay = Sunday;
 else if (strcmpi(pszDay, "Monday") == 0)
   m_eDay = Monday;
 else if (strcmpi(pszDay, "Tuesday") == 0)
   m_eDay = Tuesday;
 else if (strcmpi(pszDay, "Wednesday") == 0)
   m_eDay = Wednesday;
 else if (strcmpi(pszDay, "Thursday") == 0)
   m_eDay = Thursday;
 else if (strcmpi(pszDay, "Friday") == 0)
   m_eDay = Friday;
 else if (strcmpi(pszDay, "Saturday") == 0)
m_eDay = Saturday;
 else {
   m_eDay = Sunday;
   ok = FALSE;
 }

 return ok;
}

char* Days::getDay()
{
 switch (m_eDay) {
```

```
      case Sunday:
        strcpy(m_pszDay, "Sunday");
        break;
      case Monday:
        strcpy(m_pszDay, "Monday");
        break;
      case Tuesday:
        strcpy(m_pszDay, "Tuesday");
        break;
      case Wednesday:
        strcpy(m_pszDay, "Wednesday");
        break;
      case Thursday:
        strcpy(m_pszDay, "Thursday");
        break;
      case Friday:
        strcpy(m_pszDay, "Friday");
        break;
      case Saturday:
        strcpy(m_pszDay, "Saturday");
        break;
  }
  return m_pszDay;
}

void Days::nextDay()
{
  if (m_eDay == Saturday)
    m_eDay = Sunday;
  else
    m_eDay = weekDays(m_eDay + 1);
}

void Days::prevDay()
{
  if (m_eDay == Sunday)
    m_eDay = Saturday;
  else
    m_eDay = weekDays(m_eDay - 1);
}

void Days::addDays(unsigned uMoreDays)
{
  uMoreDays = uMoreDays % 7 + 1;
  while (uMoreDays > 0) {
    nextDay();
    uMoreDays-;
  }
}
```

This example declares the class Days, which contains the public
nested enumerated type Logical and the protected enumerated
type weekDays. The latter type lists the names of the weekdays.

Notice that the class also declares the protected weekDays-type data member m_eDay and the string data member m_pszDay. The class Days also declares the following public members:

✦ The constructor, which assigns an initial day to the data member m_eDay.

✦ The member function assignDay(), which translates the name of a weekday into an enumerator. If the function succeeds, it returns Days::TRUE. Otherwise, the function yields Days::FALSE.

✦ The member function getDay(), which returns the name of the day in data member m_eDay.

✦ The member functions nextDay() and prevDay(), which set the data member m_eDay to the next and previous day, respectively.

✦ The member function addDays(), which increments the day in data member m_eDay by uMoreDays days.

Nested structures

C++ enables you to declare structures that are nested inside classes. These structures primarily support the host class. You can make these structures available to nonmember functions if you declare them as public. In this case, you need to qualify the name of the nested structure with the name of the host class.

The following is an example of a class that has a nested structure:

```
class RescueGame
{
  public:
    RescueGame(int nMaxAttempts = 100);
    void Play();

  protected:
    // nested structure
    struct Point {
        int m_nX;
        int m_nY;
    };

    Point m_LostPersonLoc;    // location of lost
    person
    Point m_YourLoc; // location of rescuer
    int m_nNumAttempts;
    int m_nMaxAttempts;

    bool bisFound();
    void initGame();
    Point AskForNewLoc();
```

```
    void MoveTo(Point newLoc);
    double GetDistance();
};
```

This example declares the class RescueGame, which simulates
rescuing a lost person. Notice that the class declares a public
constructor and the public member function Play(). The class
declares the following items in the protected section:

+ The nested structure Point. This structure has the int-type
  members m_nX and m_nY, which store the a location.

+ The Point-type data member m_LostPersonLoc, which
  stores the location of the lost person.

+ The Point-type data member m_YourLoc, which stores the
  location of the rescuing person.

+ The int-type data member m_nNumAttempts, which stores
  the number of rescue attempts.

+ The int-type data member m_nMaxAttempts, which stores
  the maximum number of rescue attempts.

+ The bool-type member function bisFound(). This member
  returns true if you found the lost person.

+ The member function initGame(), which initializes the
  game.

+ The member function AskForNewLoc(), which prompts you
  for a new search location. This member returns a Point-type
  result.

+ The member function MoveTo(), which moves the search
  location to the coordinates that are specified by the Point-
  type parameter newLoc.

+ The member function GetDistance(), which returns the
  distance between you and the lost person.

This example shows that a class can use a nested structure to
declare data members, the result of a member function, and the
parameter of a member function.

Operators

C++ enables you to declare operators in a class. These operators
are essentially member functions that have a special declaration
and usage syntax. The C++ operators empower you to support
more abstract and natural syntax. For example, you can create a
string class and define the operators = and +=, which assign and
concatenate strings and characters.

Declaring operators

The general syntax for declaring an operator in a class is as follows:

```
class className
{
  // declaration of members
  className& operator operatorSymbol(parameterList);
};
```

The declaration of an operator uses the keyword *operator* followed by the operator's symbol. The general syntax for defining an operator is as follows:

```
className& className::operator
    operatorSymbol(parameterList)
{
  // statements
  return *this;
};
```

The definition of an operator also uses the keyword `operator`. C++ enforces rules on the number of parameters and the general category of their types. The following is a list of examples for the rules:

✦ The operator `[]` can have only one integer-compatible parameter.

✦ The assignment operators =, +=, -=, /=, *=, %=, and so on can have only one parameter. There is no restriction on the type of parameter as long as you can convert that type to the host class.

✦ The operator `( )` may have any number and type of parameters.

The following is an example of a class that declares operators:

```
class myComplex
{
  public:
  myComplex();
  // declaration of other members

  myComplex& operator =(myComplex& C);
  myComplex& operator =(double fReal);
  myComplex& operator +=(myComplex& C);
  myComplex& operator +=(double fReal);
  // declaration of other members
  protected:
  double m_fReal;
  double m_fImag;
};
```

```
myComplex& operator =(myComplex& C)
{
 m_fReal = C.m_fReal;
 m_fImag = C.m_fImag;
 return *this;
}
```

This example shows the class myComplex with the overloaded operators = and +=. The first version of the operator = has a myComplex& type, enabling it to assign one class instance to another. Then the second version assigns a double-type value to a class instance. Similarly, the overloaded operators += add class instance and floating-point numbers to class instances. The previous example also shows the definition of the operator =(myComplex). Notice that the definition has the return *this statement, which returns the reference to the targeted class.

Friend operators

In addition to friend functions, C++ supports *friend operators.* These operators have the advantage of allowing the first parameter to be of a type other than the befriended class. The following source code illustrates the limitations of member operators:

```
class myComplex
{
 public:
 myComplex();
 // declaration of other members

 myComplex& operator =(myComplex& C);
 myComplex& operator =(double fReal);
 myComplex& operator +(myComplex& C);
 myComplex& operator +(double fReal);
 // declaration of other members
};
```

This example declares the overloaded versions of the operator + as members (and not as friends) of class myComplex. Using either version of the operator + requires that the left operand be an instance of the class myComplex. The right argument can be either another class instance or a double-type value. What if you needed to write an expression in which the first operand is a double-type value and not an instance of class myComplex? You can't! This is where friend operators come in handy.

The general syntax for declaring a friend operator is as follows:

```
class className
{
 // declaration of members
 friend returnType operator
   operatorSymbol(parameterList);
};
```

The declaration of an operator uses the keywords friend and operator followed by the operator's symbol. As with friend functions, the parameter list of a friend operator must include a parameter that has the befriended class. The general syntax for defining an operator is as follows:

```
returnType operator operatorSymbol(parameterList)
{
  // statements
  return *this;
};
```

The definition of an operator uses only the keyword operator.

Applying the friend operator to the last version of class myComplex generates the following declaration:

```
class myComplex
{
  public:
  myComplex();
  // declaration of other members

  myComplex& operator =(myComplex& C);
  myComplex& operator =(double fReal);
  friend myComplex operator +(myComplex& C1,
    myComplex& C2);
  friend myComplex operator +(myComplex& C, double
    fReal);
  friend myComplex operator +(double fReal,
    myComplex& C);
  // declaration of other members
};
```

This example shows that the class myComplex declares three versions of the overloaded friend operator + to handle all possible combinations of adding class instances and doubles. Each friend operator has at least one parameter that is a class instance.

Static Members

When you create a class instance, that instance has its own copy of the data members of the class. This feature allows each instance to maintain its own information separate from other class instances. There are cases when you need data members to conceptually belong to the class and not to any particular instance. C++ supports this feature by offering static data members. Therefore, while there are as many copies of nonstatic data members as there are instances, there is only one copy of a static data member, regardless of the number of class instances. In fact, the static data members of a class exist and are accessible even if you have not yet created any instances of that class.

What are static data members good for? Static data members essentially serve classes whose instances need to or can (for the sake of saving memory space) share information. The following are several cases where you can use static data members in a class:

✦ *Counting the number of class instances.* In this case, the static data member keeps track of the number of instances. The constructors and destructors of the class need to increment and decrement, respectively, the value of such to the instance counter.

✦ *Shared information.* The static data members in a class can support a miniature database that provides common information to the class instances (such as general constants that are shared by all class instances). Therefore, using static data members can eliminate redundant information and save space.

✦ *Iterators.* You can use a static data member that stores a linked list for all of the class instances and then process all these instances.

✦ *Shared error status.* You can use static data members to consolidate managing logical errors that occur while invoking member functions.

✦ *Instance communication.* The static data members of a class can support the interaction between two or more class instances.

Declaring static data members

The general syntax for declaring a static data member is as follows:

```
static type memberName;
```

The declaration of a static data member starts with the keyword *static* and is followed by the member's type and name. The following is an example of declaring a static data member:

```
class Rectangle
{
 public:
  Rectangle()
    { m_nNumInstances++; }
  ~Rectangle()
    { m_nNumInstances-; }

  // other members

 protected:
  static int m_nNumInstances;
};
```

This example declares the class Rectangle, which contains the static data member m_nNumInstances. This data member counts the number of class instances. Therefore, the constructor and destructor increment and decrement, respectively, the value of the static data member.

Initializing static data members

The previous source code shows you how to declare a static data member and shows you how the constructor and destructor alter the values of that data member. You may have expected the constructor to initialize, rather than increment, the value of the static data member. But then, if static data members exist regardless of the number of class instances, such an initialization is inappropriate. C++ requires you to initialize static data members *outside* the class declaration. The general syntax for initializing a static data member is as follows:

```
type className::memberName = initialValue;
```

The member functions of a class access static data members just like nonstatic data members. Nonmember functions [such as the function main()] can access the public static data members by using the class name as a qualifier (that is, by using the syntax className::staticMemberName). These nonmember functions can also access public static data members by using the names of *any* class instance.

The following is an example initializing a static data member:

```
class Rectangle
{
  public:
    Rectangle()
      { m_nNumInstances++; }
    ~Rectangle()
      { m_nNumInstances-; }

    // other members

  protected:
    static int m_nNumInstances;
};

int Rectangle::m_nNumInstances = 0;
```

This example declares the class Rectangle, which contains the static data member m_nNumInstances. The last code line initializes the static data member outside the class declaration, as required by C++.

Static member functions

C++ offers static member functions to access nonpublic static data members. Most cases rarely use public static data members. Instead, classes typically declare static data members as protected and use static member functions to access them.

The general syntax for declaring a static member function is as follows:

```
static returnType functionName(parameterList);
```

The declaration of a static data member starts with the keyword static and is followed by the function's return type, function name, and optional parameter list. C++ requires that static member functions not access nonstatic data members. This is because you can use static member functions when there are no class instances — there are no copies of nonstatic data members in memory.

The following is an example of declaring a static member function:

```
class Rectangle
{
 public:
  Rectangle()
    { m_nNumInstances++; }
  ~Rectangle()
    { m_nNumInstances-; }
  static int getNumInstances()
    { return m_nNumInstances; }
  // other members

 protected:
  static int m_nNumInstances;
};

int Rectangle::m_nNumInstances = 0;
```

This example declares the class Rectangle, which contains the static data member m_nNumInstances and the static member function getNumInstances(). The static member function returns the value of the static data member.

Part XIII

Advanced OOP

In this part, you take a look at the more advanced aspects of using classes. These aspects include declaring a hierarchy of classes that you can use to create new classes by building on existing ones. This part also covers virtual functions and how they support consistent response in class hierarchies. In addition, I show you how abstract classes work and how you can better plan class hierarchies with them. Moreover, you figure out the multiple inheritance scheme and how you can use it to create sophisticated classes from separate class hierarchies. This part also covers overloading member functions and operators in a class to support sophisticated operations.

In this part . . .

- ✔ **Declaring abstract classes**
- ✔ **Declaring a class hierarchy**
- ✔ **Working with multiple inheritance**
- ✔ **Using namespace**
- ✔ **Overloading member functions and operators**
- ✔ **Using virtual functions**

Abstract Classes

In C++, not all classes need to be working classes. In fact, C++ supports abstract classes that mainly set the specifications for its descendant classes. The compiler does not enable you to create instances of an abstract class. You can place abstract classes in the root of a class hierarchy and even in a subhierarchy. You can also build a class hierarchy by using abstract classes as the base class and first sibling descendant classes. Furthermore, you can use abstract classes as the parent class deep inside a hierarchy.

Declaring an abstract class is straightforward. You need to declare at least one virtual member function by using the following syntax:

```
virtual returnType functionName(parameterList) = 0;
```

This syntax declares a virtual member function and includes = 0 to signal to the compiler that this member function has no definition and is therefore a member of an abstract class. Not all member functions of an abstract class lack definitions. You can have abstract classes that define some of their member functions to invoke the not-yet-defined member functions. The descendant classes define the latter member functions and can, therefore, use the fully defined member functions inherited from the abstract classes.

The following is an example of an abstract class and a nonabstract descendant class:

```
class AbstractRandomNumber
{
 public:
 virtual double getRandom() = 0;
 void testRandom(int nNumObs, double& fMean, double
   fSdev);
};

class RandomNumber : public AbstractRandomNumber
{
 public:
 RandomNumber()
 { m_fSeed = 13; }
 virtual double getRandom();

 protected:
 double m_fSeed;
};

void AbstractRandomNumber::testRandom(int nNumObs,
 double& fMean, double fSdev);
{
 // statements that use member function getRandom
}
```

```
double RandomNumber::getRandom()
{
  // statements
}
```

This example shows the abstract class AbstractRandomNumber, which declares the virtual member function getRandom() and the member function testRandom(). The declaration of the virtual member function indicates that the class AbstractRandomNumber does not define it. However, that class does define the member function testRandom(). The example also shows the descendant class RandomNumber, which declares and defines the virtual member function getRandom(). The descendant class inherits the member function testRandom().

Declaring a Class Hierarchy

C++ enables you to declare a descendant class from a parent class. The general syntax for declaring a descendant class that uses the single inheritance scheme is as follows:

```
class className : [public] parentClassName
  {
  [public:
  // public constructors
  // public destructor
  // public data members
  // public member functions
  ]

  [protected:
  // protected constructors
  // protected destructor
  // protected data members
  // protected member functions
  ]

  [private:
  // private constructors
  // private destructor
  // private data members
  // private member functions
  ]
  };
```

Declaring a class starts with the keyword class and is followed by the following items:

✦ The name of the class

✦ The colon character

✦ The optional keyword `public`

✦ The name of the parent class

The keyword `public` enables the class instances to access the public members of the parent class. Without this keyword, only the member functions of the descendant class can access the parent's members.

C++ enforces the following rules regarding the public, protected, and private sections of a descendant class:

✦ All the member functions can access all data members in a class regardless of which section they appear in.

✦ The class instances can access only the public members.

✦ The member functions of a descendant class can access only public and protected members of the parent class. Therefore, the private members of a class cannot be accessed by the member functions of a descendant class.

The following is an example declaring a descendant class:

```
class Rectangle
{
 public:
    Rectangle(double fLength = 0, double fWidth = 0)
      { setDimensions(fLength, fWidth); }
    void setDimensions(double fLength = 0, double
    fWidth = 0)
    {
       m_fLength = fLength;
       m_fWidth = fWidth;
    }
    double getLength()
      { return m_fLength; }
    double getWidth()
      { return m_fWidth; }
    double getArea()
      { return m_fLength * m_fWidth; }

 protected:
    double m_fLength;
    double m_fWidth;
};

class Solid : public Rectangle
{
 public:
    Solid(double fLength = 0, double fWidth = 0,
          double fHeight = 0)
      { setDimensions(fLength, fWidth, fHeight); }
```

```
    void setDimensions(double fLength = 0, double
      fWidth = 0, double fHeight = 0)
    {
      m_fLength = fLength;
      m_fWidth = fWidth;
      m_fHeight = fHeight;
    }
    double getHeight()
      { return m_fHeight; }
    double getVolume()
      { return m_fHeight * getArea(); }

  protected:
    double m_fHeight;
};
```

This example declares the base class Rectangle and its descendant class Solid. The class Rectangle declares the protected double-type data members m_fLength and m_fWidth. These data members store the length and width of a rectangle, respectively. The class declares the following public members:

+ The constructor, which initializes the data members

+ The member function setDimensions(), which assigns new values to the data members

+ The member function getLength(), which returns the value in the data member m_fLength

+ The member function getWidth(), which returns the value in the data member m_fWidth

+ The member function getArea(), which returns the area of the rectangle, calculated by using the data members

The example also declares the class Solid as a public descendant of the class Rectangle. The descendant class declares the protected double-type data member m_fHeight, which stores the height of the solid. Notice that the class inherits the protected data members m_fLength and m_fWidth and ends up with three data members. The class Solid also declares the following public members:

+ The constructor, which initializes the data members.

+ The member function setDimensions(), which assigns new values to the data members. This member function is a new version that assigns values to the inherited and declared data members.

+ The member function getHeight, which returns the value in the data member m_fHeight.

◆ The member function getVolume, which returns the volume of the solid shape, calculated by using data member m_fHeight and the result of the inherited member function getArea().

The class Solid inherits the member functions setDimensions(double, double) (which assigns values to the inherited data members), getLength(), getWidth(), and getArea(). The definition of member function getVolume() uses the inherited member function getArea().

Multiple Inheritance

C++ enables you to declare a descendant class from multiple parent classes by using the following general syntax:

```
class className : [virtual] [public]
    parentClassName1,
[virtual] [public] parentClassName2,
[other classes]
  {
[public:
// public constructors
// public destructor
// public data members
// public member functions
]

[protected:
// protected constructors
// protected destructor
// protected data members
// protected member functions
]

[private:
// private constructors
// private destructor
// private data members
// private member functions
]
  };
```

Declaring a descendant class starts with the keyword *class* and is followed by the following items:

◆ The name of the class

◆ The colon character

◆ The name of the first parent class, which is superseded by the optional keywords virtual and public

◆ A comma character

+ The name of the second parent class, which is superseded by the optional keywords `virtual` and `public`

+ A comma character

+ The name of other parents classes, with each superseded by the optional keywords `virtual` and `public`

The keyword `virtual` tells the compiler that the descendant class has parent classes that share common ancestor classes. Therefore, the keyword `virtual` alerts the compiler to that fact and permits it to anticipate common class ancestry. The keyword `public` enables the class instances to access the public members of the parent class. Without this keyword, only the member functions of the descendant class can access the parent's members. C++ enables you to declare the descendant class as a public or nonpublic descendant of the various parent classes.

The following is an example of declaring a descendant class from independent parent classes:

```
class Salary
{
 // declaration of members
};

class Person
{
 // declaration of members
};

class Employee : public Person, public Salary
{
 // declaration of members
};
```

This example shows the skeleton declarations of three classes: `Salary`, `Person`, and `Employee`. The first two classes are nondescendant classes, whereas the class `Employee` is a public descendant of both classes `Person` and `Salary`.

Suppose that the classes `Salary` and `Person` were descendants of some basic class — call it `CObject`. The declaration of the preceding classes, which now share a common ancestor class, becomes as follows:

```
class CObject
{
 // declaration of members
};
```

(continued)

(continued)

```
class Salary : virtual public CObject
{
 // declaration of members
};

class Person : virtual public CObject
{
 // declaration of members
};

class Employee : virtual public Person, virtual
    public Salary
{
 // declaration of members
};
```

These declarations use the keyword `virtual` in declaring all descendant classes, because these classes share the same base class, `CObject`. Without using the keyword `virtual` you get a compiler error.

Namespace

The namespace is a new C++ feature that solves name conflicts. Until this feature became available in compilers, C++ programs had only one namespace. The *namespace* gives classes, variables, and types a background name, if you want, that can separate them from similar names defined in other namespaces.

To declare a namespace, you should use a name that has not been previously used as a global name. The following is an example:

```
namespace Namir {// Namir is the name of this
    namespace
enum bool { false, true, dontCare };
enum Weekday { Sun, Mon, Tue, Wed, Thu, Fri, Sat };
}
```

This example uses the keyword *namespace* to declare the namespace `Namir`. This namespace declares, as an example, the enumerated types `bool` and `Weekday`. To use the names in the namespace `Namir`, I can use `Namir::` to qualify the enumerated types. Refer to the following example:

```
Namir::bool bOk = Namir::false;
Namir::Weekday myDay = Namir::Sun;
```

This example declares the variable `bOk` by using the enumerated type `Namir::bool` and initializes the variable by using the value `Namir::false`. Notice that both the type and the initial value use

Namir:: to qualify them. Likewise, the example declares the variable myDay by using the enumerated type Namir::WeekDay and initializes that variable by using the enumerator Namir::Sun.

C++ offers the directive using, which enables you to select the current namespace. The following is an example:

```
using namespace Namir; // using the namespace Namir
bool bOk = false;
Weekday myDay = Sun;
```

Notice that in the preceding example, the first statement tells the compiler that you are using the namespace Namir. The two declarations refer to the enumerated types and enumerators that are declared in that namespace without having to qualify them with Namir::.

Overloading Member Functions and Operators

C++ enables you to overload member functions and operators, because it regards member functions and operators as special functions that belong to classes. The same rules for overloading ordinary functions work with member functions and operators.

Virtual Functions

Virtual functions enable class hierarchies to offer consistent (and appropriate) response. For example, if you have a hierarchy of classes that draw various graphical shapes (points, lines, rect-angles, circles, and so on), each class has a member function Draw() that draws the shape. The classes should have the same parameter list for the member function Draw() to support a consistent response. Moreover, these functions need to be declared as virtual. The following example shows why declaring a member function as virtual supports the correct and consistent response. Examine the following code:

```
class A
{
 public:
 int doA()
 { return doA1() * doA2(); }
 int doA1()
 { return 2; }
```

(continued)

(continued)

```
int doA2()
  { return 10; }
};
class B : public A
{
 public:
 int doA1()
  { return 20; }
}

main()
{
 B objB;

 cout << objB.doA();

 return 0;
}
```

This example declares the class A and its descendant class B. The class A contains the member functions doA(), doA1(), and doA2(). Notice that the member function doA() returns a value that is the product of invoking the member functions doA1() and doA2(). The class B declares its own version of member function doA1() and inherits the member functions doA() and doA2().

When the function main() sends the C++ message doA() to object objB() (an instance of class B), what value does that message yield? Because class B declares its own version of member function doA2(), you expect the C++ message doA() to invoke the member functions B::doA1() and A::doA2(), yielding the value 200. However, the output statement in function main() displays 20, because the C++ message doA() ends up invoking the member functions A::doA1() and A::doA2(). In other words, the compiler does not get the message that you want to invoke the member function B::doA1() when you send the C++ message doA() to the instances of class B.

To solve this problem, C++ enables you to declare virtual functions. The general syntax for declaring a virtual member function is as follows:

```
virtual returnType functionName(parameterList);
```

Applying this syntax and to the classes A and B, you can generate the following code, which works correctly:

```
class A
{
 public:
 int doA()
  { return doA1() * doA2(); }
```

```
virtual int doA1()
{ return 2; }
int doA2()
{ return 10; }

};

class B : public A
{
 public:
 virtual int doA1()
 { return 20; }
};

main()
{
 B objB;

 cout << objB.doA();

 return 0;
}
```

This code declares the member function doA1() as virtual in both classes A and B. When the function main() sends the C++ message doA() to object objB, it invokes the member functions B::doA1() and A::doA2(); this yields the correct result of 200.

C++ requires you to observe the following rules with virtual member functions:

✦ A virtual member function can override a nonvirtual member function that is inherited from a parent class.

✦ You can override a virtual member function only by using another virtual member function in a descendant class. (This rule is sometimes called *once virtual, always virtual.*) The overriding member function must have the same parameter list and return type as the one being overridden.

✦ You may overload a virtual member function with a nonvirtual member function in a class. However, the descendants of that class can inherit only the virtual member function.

Techie Talk

Argument: The value that is assigned to a parameter when you call a function or a member function.

Array: A special variable that stores multiple values.

Array element: A single value in an array that is accessed by using one or more indices.

ASCIIZ: A string that stores readable characters and ends with a null character.

Base class: A class that is not a descendant of any other classes.

Catch: Responding to a runtime error (exception).

Class: A special kind of user-defined type that represents the attributes and operations of a category of objects. A class typically contains data members and member functions.

Class hierarchy: A family of classes in which some or most classes derive from one or more parent classes.

Class instance: An object that is an example of a class.

Compiler directive: A special instruction to the compiler itself.

Condition: A logical expression.

Constant: A name that is associated with a value that remains fixed during program execution.

Constructor: A special member function that initializes a class instance. C++ supports default, copy, and custom constructors.

Copy constructor: A constructor that creates a new instance by using the values in an existing one.

Custom constructor: A constructor that is neither a default nor a copy constructor.

Data member: A member of class that stores an attribute of an object.

Data type: A kind of information.

Decision-making: The capability to examine a condition and take action.

Default argument: A default value that is associated with a parameter. This kind of argument is used by the compiler when you call a function or member function and explicitly omits the value for the parameter that has a default value.

Default constructor: A constructor with no parameters or with parameters that all have default arguments. Also called a *void constructor.*

Descendant class: A class that is created as a child of another class.

Destructor: A special member function that is automatically invoked to remove a class instance.

do-while loop: A loop that iterates while a condition is true.

Dynamic variable: A variable, structure, or object that is created at runtime by using the operator `new`.

Enumerated type: A user-defined type that contains a list of names called *enumerators*. Each enumerator is a constant that has a value associated with it.

Enumerator: A value in an enumerated type.

Exception: An error that occurs during program execution.

Expression: A collection of operators and values that yields a single result.

Floating-point number: A number with a fractional part.

for loop: A loop that typically iterates for a fixed number of times.

Function call: Invoking a function.

Function overloading: Using the same name to declare multiple functions, each with a unique parameter list.

Garbage collection: A feature in a programming language that automatically reclaims dynamic variables when they reach the end of their scope. C++ does not perform garbage collection.

Identifier: A name of a program component.

if statement: A decision-making statement that supports single, dual, or multiple alternatives (by nesting an if statement).

Instance: See *class instance*.

Loop: A program part that enables you to repeat one or more tasks.

Member function: A member of a class that supports an operation of a class.

Message: The invocation of a member function with a specific class instance.

Multiple inheritance: A scheme for creating a class hierarchy where a descendant class has two or more parent classes.

Object: An instance of a class.

Operator: A symbol or name that takes a value and yields a result.

Parameter: A special variable that passes information from (and often to) a function or a member function.

Recursive function: A function that calls itself.

Send a message: Invoke a member function with a specific class instance.

Single inheritance: A scheme for creating a class hierarchy where each descendant class has only one parent class.

Static member: A class member that conceptually belongs to the class itself instead of any class instance.

String: A set of characters that store text.

Structure: A kind of user-defined type that stores data members only. Each data member has its own data type.

Switch statement: A decision-making statement that supports multiple alternatives.

Template: A general kind of code.

Template class: A class that works with one or more general data types. You must instantiate a template class before you use it with a specific data type.

Template function: A function that works with one or more general data types. You must instantiate a template function before you use it with a specific data type.

Throw: Raising a runtime error (exception).

Typecasting: Converting the value of one data type to another.

Union: A user-defined type that has data members occupying the same memory space.

Variable: A name that is associated with a value that can change during program execution.

Virtual member function: A member function that has the same parameter list as the ones in parent and/or descendant classes. Virtual member functions support consistent response in class hierarchies, enabling each class to respond in a similar way.

Void constructor: A constructor with no parameters or with parameters that all have default arguments. Also called a *default constructor.*

while loop: A loop that iterates as long as a condition is true.

Index

A

A class, 208–209
A::doA1() member function, 208
A::doA2() member function, 208–209
abstract classes, 200–201
AbstractRandomNumber class, 201
add (+) operator, 28
add (+=) assignment operator, 29
add() function, 140
addDays() member function, 190
address of (&) operator, 38, 126
addresses, storing, 118–119
Age variable, 51–52, 54
aliases
  data types, 21, 88–89
  multidimensional arrays, 22, 89–90
  single-dimensional arrays, 22, 89–90
  variables, 22–23
AND bit-manipulation assignment (&=)
    operator, 33
anInt parameter, 136
aNum int-type variable, 42
AreaType data type, 21, 89
arguments, 134–142, 211
  default, 134–135, 212
  passing by pointer, 120–123
  passing by reference, 135–136
  strings as, 136–137
arithmetic operators, 28
arithmetic with pointers, 125
ARRAY1.CPP program listing, 112–113
ARRAY2.CPP program listing, 107–109
ArrayIndexType data type, 21, 89
arrayPtr pointer, 102–103
arrays, 99, 211
  accessing elements with pointers, 125–126
  array names as pointers, 124–125
  declaring function pointer arrays, 117–118
  dynamic, 35–38, 100–103
  elements, 211
  multidimensional, 103–110
  passing as function parameters, 123–124
  pointers as function parameters, 123–124
  pointers to, 124–126
  single-dimensional, 110–113
ARRAY_SIZE constant, 9
ARRAY_SIZE identifier, 14
ASCIIZ strings, 150, 211
AskForNewLoc() member function, 187, 191

assignDay() member function, 190
assignment (=) operator, 28–29
  shallow copy, 97
AUTOEXEC.BAT file, opening, 44
automatic data type conversions, 39

B

B class, 208–209
B::doA1() member function, 208–209
backslash (\\) characters, 16, 79
backspace (\b) characters, 16, 79
bad_alloc class, 178
bad_cast class, 178
bad_typeid class, 178
base classes, 211
beep (\a) characters, 16, 79
BinarySearch() member function, 170
bisFound() member function, 191
bIsOdd variable, 78
bit manipulation operators, 33
bitwise AND (&) operator, 33
bitwise NOT (~) operator, 33
bitwise OR (|) operator, 33, 43
bitwise shift left (<<) operator, 33
bitwise shift right (>>) operator, 33
bitwise XOR (^) operator, 33
bOK variable, 206
bool data type, 78
Boolean operators, 29–32
Borland C++, 15
Borland C++ Builder, 15
break statement, 58–60, 66–69
bUseInitMatrix parameter, 109

C

c parameter, 157, 182
C versus C++, 6
C++
  basics, 5–16
  versus C, 6
capitalizing strings, 154
carriage return (\r) characters, 16, 79
case labels, 58, 61–62
catch clauses, 180–181, 211
catching exceptions, 177, 180–181
cCharSet variable, 159
cDriveName variable, 38

char data type, 19, 78–80
char-type variables, 24, 26
character literals, 78–80
characters, 78–80
  escape sequence, 79
  finding, 156–159
  sending to screen, 7–8
CHARTYPE.CPP program listing, 79–80
Choice variable, 61
cin object, 42
class keyword, 166, 201, 204
classes, 6, 163, 211
  abstract, 200–201
  constructors, 164–166
  data members, 170–171, 177, 183
  data members in public section, 169
  declaring, 166–169
  declaring data member, 167
  declaring hierarchy, 201–204
  descendant, 201–206
  destructors, 175–177
  exceptions, 177–181
  friend functions, 182–183
  hierarchy, 211
  instances, 172–175, 212
  member functions, 167–171, 183–186
  members, 167
  multiple inheritance, 204–206
  nested, 186–187
  nested enumerated types, 187–190
  nested structures, 190–191
  operators, 191–194
  pointers to, 129–130
  private section, 166–167, 170–171
  protected section, 166–167, 170
  public section, 166–167, 169
  references to, 23
  skeleton, 177
  static data members, 194–196
  static member functions, 197
  virtual functions, 207–209
cLetter variable, 39
close() member function, 42–43
closing file stream buffer, 42–43
cName array, 111, 124
cName variable, 161
cNameArray array, 105
cNameArray matrix, 105
CObject class, 205–206
Color data type, 89
colors enumerated type, 90
comma (,) operator, 33
comments, 8
  multiple-line (/* */), 8
  one-line (//), 6–8
comparing strings, 150–153

compiler, 14–15
  compiling one of multiple sets of
    statements, 10–11
  reading source–code file, 13
  syntax errors, 10
compiler directives, 8–14, 212
compiling programs, 14–15
ComplexObj object, 129
ComplexVar variable, 131
concatenating strings, 153–154
condition, 212
conditional assignment (?:)
    operator, 29–30
conditional loops, 64–66, 73–76
console output, 42
console output object, 7
const keyword, 18, 90, 120–121, 123
CONST.CPP program listing, 19–20
constant pointers, 116
constants, 17–20, 212
  associating literal values with, 9
  changing, 14
  data type associated with, 18
  declaring, 18–19
  defining names of, 9
  double-type, 18
  enumerating set of values
    or states, 90–91
  identifier naming, 18
  naming conventions, 19
  string literal, 20
  uppercase characters, 19
  usage, 19–20
  value associated with, 18
constructors, 164–166, 212
  default, 212
continue statement, 73
converting strings, 154–155
Coord1 structured variable, 97
Coord2 structured variable, 97
copy constructor, 212
copying
  strings, 155–156
  structured variables, 96–97
count parameter, 153–154, 156
Count variable, 24
cout, 7–8
cout object, 42
CPUtype enumerated type, 91
CRITICAL_VAL constant, 68
cSearch variable, 157–158, 160
cStrDest variable, 156
cString array, 111
cString variable, 154–155, 157–160, 162
cString1 variable, 153–154
cString2 variable, 153–154
cStrSrc variable, 156

cube() function, 143
custom constructor, 212
cVowels array, 112

D

DARRAY1.CPP program listing, 101–102
data
  conversion, 98
  managing, 41
data members, 177, 183, 212
  accessing, 94–95
  class private section, 170–171
  class protected section, 170
  class public section, 169
  declaring, 167
  highly sensitive, 171
  initializing, 95–96
  static, 194–196
  unions, 98
data types, 77, 212
  aliases, 21, 88–89
  AreaType, 21, 89
  ArrayIndexType, 21, 89
  associated with constants, 18
  associating with pointer, 125
  automatic conversions, 39
  bool, 78
  byte size, 38
  char, 19, 78–80
  Color, 89
  definitions, 21
  different contexts for, 88–89
  double, 19, 21, 28, 80–83
  enumerated, 90–92
  float, 28, 80–83
  floating-point, 80–83
  int, 19, 21, 28, 83–86
  integers, 83–86
  Logical, 21
  long, 28
  long double, 80–83
  long int, 83–86
  long unsigned int, 83–86
  nested, 186–191
  NumberOfElemsType, 21, 89
  numerical, 28
  predefined, 78–88
  SalaryType, 21, 89
  short int, 83–86
  short unsigned int, 83–86
  string, 86–88
  unsigned, 28
  unsigned int, 83–86
  unsigned long int, 83–86
  unsigned short int, 83–86

void, 88
WeightType, 21, 89
dataBroker class, 170
DayNum variable, 24
Days class, 189–190
DAYS_IN_YEAR constant, 20
DEBUG identifier, 12
DEBUG_MODE identifier, 10
decision-making, 212
declaring
  array of function pointers, 117–118
  class hierarchy, 201–204
  classes, 166–169
  data members, 167
  multidimensional arrays, 104–105
  objects, 172–175
  operators, 192–193
  pointers, 116–117, 119–120
  single-dimensional arrays, 110–111
  structured variables, 94
  structures, 92–93
decrement (--) operator, 34–35
default arguments, 134–135, 212
default constructor, 212
default: clause, 59–62
#define directive, 9–10, 12, 14
defined operator, 11
_DEFINES_MINMAX_ identifier, 9
defining
  macros, 9–10
  member functions, 183–185
delete operator, 36–38, 100, 103, 177
deleting dynamic arrays, 100
descendant classes, 201–206, 212
  multiple parent classes, 204–206
destructors, 175, 212
  declaring, 176–177
digits enumerated type, 91
dir parameter, 44
directives, 7–14
  #define, 9–10, 12, 14
  #elif, 10–11
  #else, 10, 13
  #endif, 11
  #error, 10
  #if, 10–11
  #ifdef, 11–13
  #ifndef, 11–13
  #include, 13
  #undef, 12–14
divide (/) operator, 28
divide (/=) assignment operator, 29
DivideComplex() friend function, 182–183
do-while loops, 64–66, 161, 212
  endless iternation, 65
  executing statements once, 64–65

do-while loops *(continued)*
  exiting, 67
  nesting, 71
doA() member function, 208–209
doA1() member function, 208–209
doA2() member function, 208
domain_error class, 178
DOS memory segments, 118
dot (.) operator, 94
double data type, 19, 21, 28, 80–83
double quote (\") characters, 16, 79
double-precision floating point
    number, 81–82
double-type constant, 18
double-type variables, 24, 26
DOWHILE.CPP program listing, 65
Draw() member function, 207
dual-alternative if statement, 52–54
dynamic allocation operators, 35–38
dynamic arrays, 35–38, 100, 102–103
  accessing elements in, 101
  deleting, 100
  managing with constructors and
      destructors listing, 176–177
  pointers, 100
dynamic memory, 35–38
dynamic variables, 35–38, 212

E

eDay parameter, 135
#elif directive, 10, 11
#else directive, 10, 11, 13
else if clause, 55, 56, 57
else keyword, 52
Employee class, 205
#endif directive, 11
endless loops, 69
EndPoint variable, 94
enum keyword, 90
enumerated types, 90–91, 212
  colors, 90
  CPUtype, 91
  declaring variables, 92
  digits, 91
  function parameter pointers, 120–121
  nested, 187–190
  weekDay, 91–92
  weekDays, 90
enumerators, 90–91, 212
eof() member function, 44
        =) operator, 30
        Error data member, 181
        ive, 10
        ace characters, 16, 79
        ter, 136

eTomorrow parameter, 136
exception class, 178
exceptions, 212
  catching, 177, 180–181
  modeling, 177
  standard, 177
  throwing, 177–181
exiting
  functions, 137–138
  loops, 66–68
EXITLOOP.CPP program listing, 67
expressions, 212
  evaluating multiple in statements, 33
eYesterday parameter, 136

F

Factorial() function, 145
fail() member function, 44
far pointers, 118–119
fArr array, 112, 126
fBase parameter, 135
fCube array, 106
fErrorCode parameter, 135
fExponent parameter, 135
fFactor variable, 29
file stream I/O functions
  closing, 42–43
  opening, 43–44
files
  binary stream input, 46–47
  binary stream output, 45–46
  read, 9
  setting stream mode, 48
FileSize variable, 24
finding characters, 156–159
FindLostPersonGame class, 187
fInitMat matrix, 109
fInitVal parameter, 109
float data type, 28, 80–83
floating-point data types, 80–83
floating-point numbers, 213
flushing output, 42–43
fMat array, 106
fMatrix array, 104
fMatrix matrix, 105
fnewXCoord parameter, 168, 185
fnewYCoord parameter, 168, 185
FocalPoint variable, 96
for keyword, 68
for loop, 66, 68–71, 103–104, 126, 175, 213
  comma (,) operator, 33
  exiting, 67
  loop continuation test, 68
  loop control variables, 70
  loop initialization part, 68

loop update part, 69
multiple control variables, 33
nested, 71, 73
open loop, 69
upward-counting fixed loop, 70
FOR1.CPP program listing, 70
form feed (\f) characters, 16, 79
fReal parameter, 182
friend functions, 182–183
friend keyword, 182, 194
friend operators, 193–194
fScl variable, 29
fstream class, 48
fSum variable, 29
functions, 133
function pointers, declaring
    array of, 117–118
functions, 7, 133, 137
  arguments, 134–137, 140–142
  array pointers as parameters, 123–124
  body of statements, 7
  components, 146
  declaring before defining, 143–144
  default arguments, 134–135
  defining pseudo-inline, 9–10
  exiting, 137–138
  file stream I/O, 42–44
  friend, 182–183
  inline, 138–139
  invoking with pointer, 117–118
  manipulating ASCIIZ strings, 150
  member, 167–186
  overloading, 139–140, 213
  parameters, 140–142
  parameters pointers to enumerated
    types, 120–121
  parameters pointers to
    structures, 121–122
  passing arguments by reference, 135–136
  passing arrays as parameters, 123–124
  pointers as parameters, 122–123
  pointers to, 127–128
  prototyping, 143–144
  random-access I/O streaming, 44–45
  recursion, 145
  sequential binary streaming I/O, 45–47
  sequential text stream I/O, 47–48
  statement block ({}), 7
  syntax, 145–147
  template, 140
  virtual, 207–209
  void, 138, 147–148
fVector array, 110
fX variable, 29
fXchange parameter, 168, 185
fXCoord data member, 167

fXMat matrix, 109
fY variable, 29
fYchange parameter, 168, 185
fYCoord data member, 167

G

garbage collection, 213
getArea() member function, 203–204
getDay() member function, 190
GetDistance() member function, 187, 191
getHeight() member function, 203
getImag() member function, 129–130
getLength() member function, 203
getline() member function, 46–48
getNewCoord() function, 174–175
getNumInstances() static member
    function, 197
getRandom() member function, 201
getRandom() virtual member function, 201
getReal() member function, 129–130
getScreenColors() function, 120
getShiftCoord() function, 174
getShiftInCoord() function, 175
getVolume() member function, 204
getWidth() member function, 203–204
getXCoord() function, 175
getXCoord() member function, 168–169, 185
getYCoord() function, 175
getYCoord() member function, 168–169, 185
good() member function, 44
greater than (>) operator, 30
greater than or equal to (>=) operator, 30
Greet() function, 147

H

HELP constant, 19
HI constant, 32
horizontal tab (\t) characters, 16, 79
Hungarian notation, 3–4

I

i control variable, 33, 66, 69, 71, 73,
    103, 110, 113
I/O (input/output)
  file streaming functions, 42–44
  random-access streaming
    functions, 44–45
  sequential binary streaming
    functions, 45–47
IDE (integrated development
    environment), 14

identifiers
  case-sensitivity, 15
  characters, 15
  defined or not defined, 11–13
  maximum length, 15
  naming constants, 18
  naming rules, 15
  redefining, 14
  reserved words and, 15
#if directive, 10–11
if statement, 68–69, 73, 92, 213
  dual-alternative, 52–54
  multiple-alternative, 54–57
  single-alternative, 50–52
if-else statement, 52–54, 78
IF1.CPP program listing, 51
IF2.CPP program listing, 53
IF3.CPP program listing, 56–57
#ifdef directive, 11–13
IFDEF1.CPP program listing, 12
#ifndef directive, 11–13
ifstream class, 48
#include directive, 13
increment (++) operator, 34–35
indentifiers, 213
  removing definition of, 13–14
index ([]) operator, 103, 110
Index variable, 24
indirection access (*) operator, 38
infinite loops, 69
inheritance, multiple, 204–206
initGame() member function, 187, 191
initializing
  data members, 95–96
  multidimensional arrays, 103–110
  pointers, 119–120
  single-dimensional arrays, 111–113
  static data members, 196
  strings, 161
  structured variables, 95–96
inline functions, 138–139
input, 41
  basics, 42
  moving stream pointer to location of,
    44–45
input (>>) operator, 42, 47
inputChar variable, 57
instances, 213
int data type, 19, 21, 28, 83–86
int-type variable, 24, 26
integer data types, 83–86
Integer variable, 26
integers, 83–86
InterestRate variable, 24
intRange structure, 136

INTTYPE.CPP program listing, 85
invalid_argument class, 178
ios class, 44, 48
ios:: beg enumerator, 45
ios:: cur enumerator, 45
ios:: end enumerator, 45
ios::failure class, 178
IOSTREAM.H header file, 13, 42
_IOSTREAM_H_ identifier, 9
isFound() member function, 187
isNotVowel() function, 76
istream class, 44, 46

J

j control variable, 33, 50, 64, 74, 113

K

k control variable, 50, 103, 113
keyboard input, 42
keywords, 18

L

lASCII variable, 39
length_error class, 178
less than (<) operator, 30
less than or equal to (<=) operator, 30
Letter variable, 26, 76
LinearSearch() function, 118, 123–124, 128
LinearSearch() member function, 170
linkers, 14
linking programs, 14
literal characters, 85–86
literal integers, 84
literal text, 8
literal values, 9
literals, 84
LO constant, 32
LoadScreen() function, 121–122
logical AND (&&) operator, 30
Logical data type, 21
Logical enumerated type, 189
logical NOT (!) operator, 30
logical OR (||) operator, 30
logic_error class, 178
long data type, 28
long double data type, 80–83
long int data type, 83–86
long keyword, 84
long unsigned int data type, 83–86
long-type variables, 24
loop control variables, 68

loops, 63, 213
  conditional, 64–66, 73–76
  continuation test, 68
  do-while, 64–66
  endless, 69
  exiting, 66–68
  for, 66, 68–71
  infinite, 69
  initialization part, 68
  nesting, 71–73
  open, 69
  preventing endless, 69
  skipping iterations, 73
  testing condition after execution, 64–66
  testing continuation condition before
      executing, 73–76
  upward-counting fixed, 70
  while, 73–76
Lowercase() function, 10

M

macros, defining, 9–10
main() function, 7–8, 12, 26, 32, 51–52, 54,
      57, 61, 66, 68, 71, 73, 76, 78, 85, 97,
      102, 109, 113, 118, 123, 128–129, 131,
      137, 139, 142–143, 175, 181, 196, 208
Matrix object, 109
MAX constant, 9, 100, 110–111
MaxAttempts constant, 19
MAX_ATTEMPTS constant, 19
max_clients_per_day constant, 19
MAX_CLIENTS_PER_DAY constant, 19
MAX_COLS constant, 104–105, 109
MAX_COORD constant, 174
MAX_DAYS constant, 19–20
MAX_ELEMS constant, 103, 113
MAX_LINES constant, 71
MAX_MOVES constant, 175
MAX_ROWS constant, 104–105, 109
MAX_VAL constant, 68
Me variable, 94
member functions, 167–168, 183–186, 213
  class private section, 170–171
  class protected section, 170
  class public section, 169
  defining, 183–185
  overloading, 207
  static, 197
memory, conserving space, 98
messages, 213
Microsoft Visual C++, 15
MiddleInitial variable, 24
minus (-) operator, 28
MINUTES_IN_HOUR constant, 19
MINUTE_PER_HOUR constant, 9

minValue constant, 19
MIN_ELEMS constant, 103
MIN_VAL constant, 68
MIN_VALUE constant, 19
modulo (%=) assignment operator, 29
modulus (%) operator, 28
moveBy() member function, 168–169, 185
moveBy() message, 175
moveTo() member function, 168–169,
      185, 187, 191
moveTo() message, 175
multidimensional arrays
  accessing, 103–104
  aliases, 22, 89–90
  declaring, 104–105
  initializing, 105–110
multiple inheritance, 204–206, 213
multiple-alternative if statement, 54–57
multiple-alternative switch
      statement, 58–62
multiple-line (/* */) comments, 8
multiply (*) operator, 28
multiply (*=) assignment operator, 29
myArray class, 176–177
MYARRAY.HPP header file, 13
myChar variable, 53
myClass class, 36
myComplex class, 129, 182, 193–194
myComplex structure, 131
myData structure, 36
MYDATA.DAT file, 44–45
myDay variable, 92
myError1 class, 181
myError2 class, 181
myMatrix class, 109
myPersonnelData array, 124
myPoint class, 165–166
myPoint constructor, 166
myPower() function, 134–135, 140
myPowerDbl() function, 139
myRectangle variable, 94
myStringLength() function, 136–137
m_bDataIsSorted data member, 170
m_cBirthYear data member, 93
m_cFirstName data member, 93
m_cLastName data member, 93
m_cMiddleInitial data member, 93
m_eDay data member, 190
m_fHeight data member, 203–204
m_fImag data member, 129, 131
m_fLength data member, 93, 95, 203
m_fMatrix data member, 109
m_fReal data member, 129, 131
m_fWeight data member, 93
m_fWidth data member, 93, 95, 203
m_fX data member, 93, 95–98, 165
m_fXCoord data member, 169, 172, 185

m_fY data member, 93, 95–97, 165
m_fYCoord data member, 169, 172, 185
m_lfx data member, 98
m_LostPersonLoc data member, 187, 191
m_LowerLeftCorner data member, 96
m_LowerRightCorner data member, 93, 96
m_nError data member, 181
m_nErrorCode data member, 136
m_nInt data member, 98
m_nMaxAttempts data member, 191
m_nMaxVal data member, 136
m_nMinVal data member, 136
m_nNumAttempts data member, 187, 191
m_nNumInstances static data
    member, 196–197
m_nSearchDataBuffer data member, 171
m_nTheVal data member, 136
m_nX data member, 187, 191
m_nY data member, 187, 191
m_pData data member, 177
m_pszDay data member, 190
m_pszFilename data member, 177
m_UpperLeftCorner data member, 93, 95–96
m_UpperRightCorner data member, 95
m_YourLoc data member, 187, 191

N

N variable, 29
name conflicts, 206–207
namespace keyword, 206
namespaces, 206–207
naming items rules, 15
Namir::bool enumerated type, 206
Namir::WeekDay enumerated type, 207
nArr array, 112, 125
nArray array, 14, 118, 123, 128
nArr[0] element, 125
nArr[1] element, 125
nArr[2] element, 125
nASCII variable, 39
nBins variable, 29
nCharSize variable, 38
nCount variable, 29, 34–35, 118–120,
    123, 126–128, 156
nCustomerNumber variable, 142
nDriveNameSize variable, 38
near pointers, 118
nError parameter, 181
nested
    classes, 186–187
    data types, 186–191
    enumerated types, 187–190
    structures, 190–191
NESTED.CPP program listing, 72
nesting loops, 71–73

new line (\n) characters, 16, 79
new operator, 36–37, 100, 103
new point (};) operator, 38
newLine() function, 148
NEW_LINE constant, 20
next() function, 135
nextAndPrevious() function, 135
nextDay() member function, 190
nIndex variable, 159–160
nIntArr array, 111
nIntCube array, 105
nMat matrix, 106
nMax parameter, 136
nMin parameter, 136
nMode parameter, 43
nNum parameter, 136, 139, 145
nNum variable, 23, 34–35, 78, 130
nNum1 variable, 32
nNum2 variable, 32
nNum3 variable, 32
nNumber parameter, 142
nNumberOfElements parameter, 137
nNumElems variable, 103
nOffset variable, 157–158
not equal to (!=) operator, 30
nProt parameter, 43
nSearchVal variable, 118, 123, 128
nSwapBuffer variable, 113
null-terminated strings, 150
Num variable, 55–56, 59
Num1 variable, 66, 73
Num2 variable, 66, 73
Number variable, 26
NumberOfDisks variable, 24
NumberOfElemsType data type, 21, 89
numbers
    with decimals, 80–83
    double-precision floating point, 81–82
    integers, 83–86
    scientific format, 82
    single-precision floating point, 81–82
numerical data types, 28
nVal variable, 67, 181

O

objects, 213
    declaring, 172–175
    pointers to, 129–130
    sending messages to, 172
off parameter, 44
offset address, 118–119
ofstream class, 48
one-line comments (//), 6–8
open loop, 69
open() member function, 43–44

opening file stream, 43–44
operands, 28
operator keyword, 192, 194
operators, 27, 213
  arithmetic, 28
  assignment, 28–29
  bit manipulation, 33
  Boolean, 29–32
  classes, 191–194
  declaring, 192–193
  decrement (--), 34–35
  dynamic allocation, 35–38
  friend, 193–194
  increment (++), 34–35
  overloading, 207
  pointer, 38
  relational, 29–32
  sizeof, 38
OR bit-manipulation assignment (| =)
      operator, 33
orderCharacters() function, 136
Origin variable, 94
ostream class, 45
otherPoint parameter, 165
output, 41
  basics, 42
  flushing, 42–43
  moving stream pointer to
      location of, 44–45
output (<<) operator, 7–8, 42, 47
output statement, 7–8
out_of_range class, 178
overflow_error class, 178
overloading
  functions, 139–140
  member functions, 207
  operators, 207

P

parameters, 213
pArr pointer, 100
pBackgroundColor parameter, 121
pComplex pointer, 129, 131
pData parameter, 124
Person class, 205
Person structure, 93
pfArr pointer, 126
pfArray parameter, 124
pForegroundColor parameter, 120
pInt pointer, 36, 38
pIntArr pointer, 37–38
Play() member function, 187, 191
plus (+) operator, 28
pmyClass pointer, 36–37
pmyData pointer, 36

pnArr pointer, 125
pnArray parameter, 124
pnCount pointer, 117, 119–120, 126–127
pnInt1 pointer, 117
pnInt2 pointer, 117
pnNum constant pointer, 116
pnNum pointer, 130
pNum1 pointer, 119
pNum2 pointer, 119
Point class, 187
Point structure, 93, 96, 191
pointer access (->) operator, 38, 94, 130–131
pointer operators, 38
pointers, 115
  accessing array elements, 125–126
  arithmetic, 125
  array names as, 124–125
  array pointers as function
      parameters, 123–124
  arrays, 124–126
  associating data types with, 125
  classes, 129–130
  constant, 116
  declaring, 116–120
  existing variables, 126–127
  far, 118–119
  functions, 117, 127–128
  as function parameters, 122–123
  function parameters as pointers to
      enumerated types, 120–121
  function parameters as pointers to
      structures, 121–122
  initializing, 119–120
  near, 118
  objects, 129–130
  offset address, 118–119
  passing arguments, 120–123
  to pointers, 130
  reference variables vs., 131
  segment address, 119
  structures, 130–131
Points array, 94
pos parameter, 44
ppnNum pointer, 130
predefined data types, 78–88
prevDay() member function, 190
private classes, 166
private keyword, 166, 204
programs
  comments, 8
  compiling, 14–15
  creating and destroying variables
      while running, 35–38
  directive, 7
  linking, 14
  main() function, 7–8
  multiple-line (/* */) comments, 8

programs *(continued)*
  one-line comments (//), 6–8
  output statements, 7–8
  parts of, 6–8
  performing task when condition
    is true, 50–51
  return 0 statement, 8
PROMPT constant, 20
protected classes, 166
protected keyword, 166
prototyping functions, 143–144
pScreen parameter, 121–122
pseudo-inline functions, 9–10
pShape variable, 95
pStr pointer, 158, 160
pszArrayOfStrings parameter, 137
pszFilename constant pointer, 123
pszName constant pointer, 116
pszName pointer, 117, 119
public classes, 166
public keyword, 166, 202, 205

Q

question mark (\?) characters, 16, 79

R

rand() function, 32, 174
random-access stream I/O functions, 44–45
RandomNumber class, 201
range_error class, 178
read() member function, 44, 46–47
REALTYPE.CPP program listing, 81–82
recFactorial() function, 145
Reciprocal() function, 10
RECORDS.DAT file, 44
Rectangle base class, 203
Rectangle class, 196–197
Rectangle structure, 93, 96
recursion, 145
recursive functions, 213
reference variables, 22–23
  pointers versus, 131
relational operators, 29–32
RELOP1.CPP program listing, 30–31
RescueGame class, 191
reserved words and identifiers, 15
return 0 statement, 8
return statement, 137–138
reversing strings, 161–162
rNum reference variable, 23
runtime errors, 177–181
runtime_error class, 178

S

Salary class, 205
SalaryType data type, 21, 89
SaveScreen() function, 121–122
scientific number format, 82
screen, sending characters to, 7–8
ScreenChars structure, 121
Search array, 118
Search function pointer, 123
Search pointer, 123, 128
Search() function, 123
Search() member function, 170
SearchAndSave() function, 123
Search[0] pointer, 118
Search[1] pointer, 118
seekg() member function, 44–45
segment address, 119
sending messages, 213
sequential binary stream I/O, 45–47
sequential text stream I/O functions, 47–48
setComplex() member function, 129
setDimensions() member function, 203–204
setRange() function, 136
setVal() function, 136
shallow copy, 97
Shapes variable, 95
shift left bit-manipulation assignment
    (<<=) operator, 33
shift right bit-manipulation assignment
    (>>=) operator, 33
short int data type, 83–86
short keyword, 84
short unsigned int data type, 83–86
Show() function, 124
show() message, 109
show1() function, 21, 89
show2() function, 21, 89
showAndGetNextInt() function, 141–142
showChar() function, 148
showInt() function, 148
showStrings() function, 137
signed keyword, 84
single inheritance, 213
single quote (\') characters, 16, 79
single-alternative if statement, 50–52
single-dimensional arrays
  accessing, 110
  aliases, 22, 89–90
  declaring, 110–111
  initializing, 111–113
single-precision floating point
    number, 81–82
sizeof operator, 11, 38
sizeof() function, 98
skeleton classes, 177

skipping loop iterations, 73
software, flagging state, 9
Solid class, 204
Solid descendant class, 203
Sort() function, 124
special characters, 16
sqr() function, 147
Square() function, 10, 139, 143
srand() function, 32
standard exceptions, 177
StartPoint variable, 94
statement block, 50
statements, 50
  compiling one of multiple sets, 10–11
  ending with semicolon (;), 7
  evaluating multiple expressions in, 33
  output, 7–8
  return 0, 8
static data members, 194–196
static keyword, 195, 197
static member functions, 197
static members, 213
StatSearch() function, 118, 123, 128
strcat() function, 153
strchr() function, 156–157
strcmp() function, 150–151
strcpy() function, 155–156
strcspn() function, 159
stream libraries, 42, 48
streaming, 41
  basics, 42
  error in operation, 44
  error status, 44
  file I/O functions, 42–44
  moving pointer to next I/O location, 44–45
  no error in operation, 44
  not reached end of file, 44
  random-access I/O functions, 44–45
  sequential binary I/O functions, 45–47
  sequential text I/O functions, 47–48
stricmp() function, 151
string data type, 86–88
string literals, 20, 86–88
string parameter, 157, 161
STRING.H header file, 150, 153
string1 parameter, 150–156, 158–160
string2 parameter, 150–156, 158–160
strings, 86–88, 149–150, 213
  as arguments, 136–137
  ASCIIZ, 150
  capitalizing, 154
  case-insensitive comparison, 151
  case-insensitive comparison of fixed
    number of characters, 152–153
  case-sensitive comparison, 150–151
  case-sensitive comparison of fixed
    number of characters, 152

comparing, 150–153
concatenating, 153–154
converting, 154–155
copying, 155–156
  copying all characters, 155–156
  copying specified characters, 155–156
  finding characters, 156–159
  finding first character, 156–157
  finding last character, 156–158
  first character not in set, 158–159
  first character part of character set, 159
  initializing, 161
  length, 160–161
  lowercase from uppercase, 155
  null-terminated, 150
  reversing, 161–162
  substrings, 160
strlen() function, 160–161
strlwr() function, 155
strncat() function, 153–154
strncmp() function, 152
strncpy() function, 155–156
strnicmp() function, 152–153
strrchr() function, 156–158
strrev() function, 161–162
strspn() function, 158–159
strstr() function, 160
STRTYPE.CPP program listing, 86–87
structured variables
  copying, 96–97
  declaring, 94
  initializing, 95–96
structuredVariable variable, 95
structures, 92–93, 213
  accessing data members, 94–95
  declaring, 92–93
  declaring variables, 94
  function parameter pointers, 121–122
  initializing data members, 95–96
  nested, 190–191
  pointers to, 130–131
  references to as function parameters, 136
  unions, 97–98
strupr() function, 154
substrings, 160
subtract (-) operator, 28
subtract (-=) assignment operator, 29
sum variable, 64, 66, 73–74
superDataBroker class, 171
switch statement, 49, 213
  multiple-alternative, 58–62
switch variable, 58
SWITCH.CPP program listing, 60–61
Symantec C++, 15
syntax errors, 10
system programming, 33
szName parameter, 43

T

tasks
  performing when condition is true, 50–51
  repeating fixed number of times, 68–71
template classes, 214
template functions, 140, 214
templates, 214
testRandom() member function, 201
text
  input, 46
  literal, 8
  sequential text I/O functions, 47–48
textScreen array type, 89–90
textScreen matrix type, 22
throw keyword, 178–179
throw statement, 181
throwing, 214
throwing exceptions, 177–181
  catch clauses, 180–181
  throw keyword, 178–179
  try block, 179–181
true/false, 78
try block, 179–181
type definitions, 21–22
type modifier keywords, 84
typecasting, 39, 214
typedef statement, 21–22, 88–89
  newType parameter, 21, 88
  oldType parameter, 21, 88

U

#undef directive, 12–14
unions, 97–98, 214
unsigned data type, 28
unsigned int data type, 83–86
unsigned keyword, 84
unsigned long int data type, 83–86
unsigned short int data type, 83–86
UpdateScreen() function, 121–122
Uppercase() function, 10
upward-counting fixed loop, 70
Us array, 94
using directive, 207

V

values
  assigning to variable, 29
  associated with constants, 18
  storing, 23–26
VAR1.CPP program listing, 25
variableName operand, 34–35

variables, 17, 23–26, 214
  adding or subtracting one from
    value, 34–35
  aliases, 22–23
  assigning values to, 29
  byte size, 38
  char-type, 24, 26
  creating and destroying while program
    runs, 35–38
  declaring, 23–24
  declaring with enumerated types, 92
  double-type, 24, 26
  dynamic, 35–38
  int-type, 24, 26
  long-type, 24
  loop control, 68
  not initialized, 23
  pointers to existing, 126–127
  reference, 22–23
  switch, 58
vertical tab (\v) characters, 16, 79
virtual functions, 207–209
virtual keyword, 204–206
virtual member functions, 214
void constructor, 214
void data type, 88
void functions, 147–148
  return statement, 138

W

Watcom C++, 15
weekDay enumerated type, 91–92, 135
weekDays array type, 22, 89–90
weekDays enumerated type, 90, 189
WeightType data type, 21, 89
while clause, 161
while loop, 73–76, 214
  exiting, 67
  nesting, 71
  skipping statements, 74
WHILE.CPP program listing, 75
Windows 3.1 memory segments, 118
write() member function, 44–46

X

XFloat union, 98
XInt union, 98
XOR bit-manipulation assignment (^=)
    operator, 33

Y

You variable, 94

❏ YES!

Please keep me informed about IDG's World of Computer Knowledge. Send me the latest IDG Books catalog.